As one of the world's longest established
and best-known travel brands,
Thomas Cook are the experts in travel.

For more than 135 years our
guidebooks have unlocked the secrets
of destinations around the world,
sharing with travellers a wealth of
experience and a passion for travel.

**Rely on Thomas Cook as your
travelling companion on your next trip
and benefit from our unique heritage.**

Thomas Cook **traveller** guides

DEVON &
CORNWALL

Debbie Stowe

D0419942

Thomas
Cook

Written and updated by Debbie Stowe
Original photography by Vasile Szakacs

Published by Thomas Cook Publishing
A division of Thomas Cook Tour Operations Limited
Company registration no. 3772199 England
The Thomas Cook Business Park, Unit 9, Coningsby Road,
Peterborough PE3 8SB, United Kingdom
Email: books@thomascook.com, Tel: + 44 (0) 1733 416477
www.thomascookpublishing.com

Produced by Cambridge Publishing Management Limited
Burr Elm Court, Main Street, Caldecote CB23 7NU
www.cambridgepm.co.uk

ISBN: 978-1-84848-365-1

First edition © 2009 Thomas Cook Publishing
This second edition © 2011
Text © Thomas Cook Publishing
Maps © Thomas Cook Publishing/PCGraphics (UK) Limited
Contains Ordnance Survey data © Crown copyright and database right 2010

Series Editor: Karen Beaulah
Production/DTP: Steven Collins

Printed and bound in Spain by GraphyCems

Cover photography © BANANA PANCAKE/Alamy

Contents

Introduction

Miles and miles of superlative coastline, two inspiring national parks and the best weather in the country – it's little surprise that Devon and Cornwall are among the most popular tourist destinations in the United Kingdom. Throw in the culinary revolution being spearheaded by a couple of celebrity chefs, some extraordinary building conversions providing stylish accommodation, and a clutch of unique tourist attractions, and there's very little missing from the line-up.

First and foremost is the scenery, and topping the bill must be the sea views. As a peninsula, the water – be it the English Channel, Atlantic Ocean or one of the many rivers – is never far away. Not only does this often result in a vision of gorgeous, shimmering blue when you open your hotel curtains in the morning, it also brings with it the picturesque fishing trade, seemingly little changed from centuries past. The sea has also bred a wealth of stories, real and mythical, of catastrophic shipwrecks and gnarled old smugglers. Back in the here and now, surfing is just the most high-profile of the array of watersports on offer. And it's hard to beat the freshness (or, indeed, reduce the food miles, for the eco-worrier) when you can see your evening meal being hauled out of the ocean that morning.

Food, seldom celebrated as a British forte, is another of the region's highlights. As well as the catch of the day, the recent trade in organic produce gives Devon and Cornwall some of the most delectable and guilt-free fare available countrywide. Calorific but irresistible, the counties' culinary icons – the Devon cream tea and Cornish pasty – will be constant temptations as you navigate the many attractions of the region.

These attractions include both manmade and natural stop-offs that will entertain, amuse and astound. As well as being stunning locations in their own right, the two national parks and one moor afford enough activities to wear out the most energetic of travellers (including children, who will have a super time visiting Devon and Cornwall). From hiking, biking and horse riding to strolling and pub-lunching, there is plenty for everyone. Land's End is another geographical singularity that will take your breath away – and not just because it's so windy! The Eden Project symbolises the new environmentalism that is taking off all over the region, as well as being another cracking day out.

If all this outdoorsy stuff is not your cup of tea, there is a multitude of ways to pass the time without subjecting yourself to the elements. Eccentric museums on subjects ranging from witchcraft and smuggling to seafaring and the movies can absorb hours. The region's artistic traditions are also well worth some exploration, with the Tate St Ives a recognition of how important Cornwall's contribution to the UK's art scene has been. And distinctive churches and atmospheric old castles afford an exciting glimpse of the region's history.

Devon and Cornwall offer seclusion and sunshine, and for even more of the same the Isles of Scilly are just a short voyage – or scenic flight – away. Though once you've seen the peninsula itself, you may be loath to go anywhere else.

The region is home to some of England's great wildernesses, such as Dartmoor

The region

Devon and Cornwall have some of the most untamed landscapes in the country. As a peninsula, the region is blessed with reams of golden beaches and craggy cliffs, plus magnificent river, sea and ocean views. The inland area holds its own, with wild moorland, neat patchwork fields and farmland punctuated by quaint little English villages that look much like the last couple of centuries have passed them by entirely.

The two counties are England's most westward, stuck out on a long protruding cape unlike anywhere else in England. Moving southwest, from its border with Somerset, Devon narrows into Cornwall, which finally splits into two distinct peninsulas containing the country's southernmost and westernmost mainland points, respectively. It is the second of these, Land's End, which is by far the more famous, attracting tourists and charity walkers in droves.

It's easy to ascribe Devon and Cornwall distinguishing characteristics. Devon is markedly more 'English' in feel, summed up by thatched cottages, winding lanes, tidy farmland and the Devon cream tea, which consists of the über-Anglo trinity of scones, jam and a pot of tea. By contrast, its neighbour is wilder, its cultural roots bound up with the Celtic nations with which it had maritime links. Rugged and wild, its history beset with battles and unrest, Cornwall is the wayward younger child

to the more demure, older sibling that is Devon.

The sea, the sea

While differences can be sought and found, the two have enough in common to be a unified holiday destination. Most obviously, there's the coastline. Cornwall might have more of that for its size, but Devon's history is equally permeated with the maritime, perhaps embodied most in Plymouth. Ports, former fishing towns and seaside resorts, many of which are seeing pursuits piscatorial give way to the financial inducements of tourism, dot the shore and are likely to figure prominently on your schedule. And they take all manner of guises, from surfing hotspot, Riviera resort and gentrified second-home hub to bucket-n-spader magnet and workaday port.

The diversity of resorts is reflected in the cross section of visitors who travel to the region: well-heeled second-homers, bronzed surf dudes, genteel

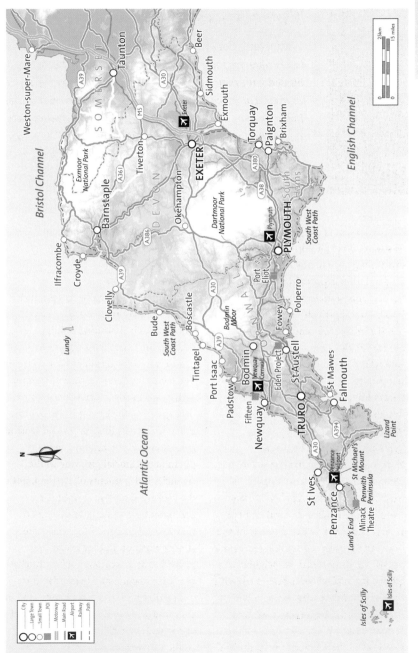

Bristol Channel

Weston-super-Mare

Taunton

Beer

Sidmouth

Exmouth

A39

A30

M5

SOMERSET

Exmoor National Park

A361

Exeter

EXETER

Torquay

Paignton

Brixham

Tiverton

A380

South Hams

A38

Barnstaple

DEVON

Okehampton

Dartmoor National Park

Plymouth

PLYMOUTH

South West Coast Path

Ilfracombe

Croyde

A386

A39

Clovelly

Bude

Boscastle

South West Coast Path

Port Isaac

Tintagel

A30

Bodmin Moor

A39

Padstow

Bodmin

Newquay Cornwall

Eden Project

Port Eliot

Fowey

Polperro

CORNWALL

St Austell

Fifteen

Newquay

TRURO

St Mawes

Falmouth

Lizard Point

A394

A30

St Ives

Penzance Heliport

St Michael's Mount

Penzance

Land's End

Minack Theatre

Penwith Peninsula

Lundy

Atlantic Ocean

English Channel

N

Isles of Scilly

Isles of Scilly

City

Large Town

Small Town

POI

Motorway

Main Road

Airport

Railway

Path

0   25km

0   15 miles

senior citizens revisiting the holiday destinations of their childhood, weekenders and foodies from the capital, young couples and families trying to holiday ethically by eschewing air travel, plus a legion of foreign tourists 'doing' the southwest on whistlestop tours of the United Kingdom.

Whichever you choose, fine views are part of the deal, and decent weather is as guaranteed as ever it can be in the UK. Nowhere else in the country enjoys as much sun, and several microclimates further boost your chances of balmy days. Of course, as an exposed peninsula, winds can also come into the equation, and many coastal days may be of the 'windswept and interesting' variety.

The region's unusual geography makes it prone to some of the UK's freak weather: floods have hit the coastal towns on more than one occasion in recent years, with the most notable being the flash floods that devastated Boscastle in August 2004. But aside from such extreme cases, the more intense weather often lends the topography an aesthetically pleasing drama.

Moorland, myth and mystery

The raw visual power of the Atlantic Ocean (and, to a lesser extent, the English Channel) has its dry-land counterpart in the three large expanses of wilderness, the moors, two of which are national parks. Dartmoor, Exmoor and Bodmin provide acres of great outdoors ripe for the exploring. This can be done on foot, pony or bike – even by car, to some extent. Yawning fields lashed by winds that seem to cry out for a Heathcliff or Darcy to charge through them on horseback, ancient monuments steeped in mystery that hark back to prehistoric rituals and dark myths, and an abundance of wildlife characterise the three great moors. Both on and off them, swathes of the region's land have been allocated to the protection of the National Trust.

The moors are one hub of the multifarious flora and fauna species that inhabit Devon and Cornwall.

Local priest and theologian Richard Hooker is commemorated outside Exeter cathedral

The rolling fields of Devon are at the forefront of British organic farming

Numerous mammals (some real, some mythical) are linked to the areas, from the celebrated ponies to deer, rabbits, badgers, foxes and rare sheep. Avian life attracted by the varied conditions includes grouse, partridge and pheasants (sometimes, unfortunately, with shooting parties in their wake). The sea is the other main centre of local wildlife. As well as the countless species of fish (many of which end up on the plate, courtesy of Rick Stein and his like) you may be lucky enough to spot dolphins and basking sharks. Seabirds, too, are plentiful. Flora consists of a staggering range, from meadow, grassland and thistle to heather, gorse and berries. On the coast, beaches are punctuated by dramatic granite cliffs and sand dunes.

Feeding frenzy

Some of the terrain has been given over to cultivation, and farmland makes up a significant portion of the counties. Fields of gambolling lambs will be another amiably pastoral recurring feature of your trip. Devon, in particular, is at the forefront of organic farming in the UK. Perhaps because the economic engine of both counties is now tourism, and that is entirely contingent on a pristine outdoor environment, eco-thinking is now at the heart of the peninsula's philosophy. With big players like the National Trust and Duchy of Cornwall leading the way, concepts like 'organic' and 'food miles' are filtering down the chain (despite the pressures of the financial crisis), with many local businesspeople trumpeting the local

The Eden Project is a unique attraction

Rural idyll

Both in and outside the parks, Devon and Cornwall's populated areas often take the form of bucolic villages. Thatched roofs, watermills and old inns set the tone, with some of the smaller hamlets consisting of just a few cottages. Settlements – such a traditional word seems appropriate – are often linked by snaking country lanes (the sort that have names in the local dialect, like *bownder* or *ope*), flanked by enormous hedgerows. Even the average-sized towns typically have a sprinkling of cottages that endeavour to preserve the rural atmosphere in the face of the relentless march of suburbanisation.

The same can even be said of some of the bigger residential areas. Of Devon and Cornwall's three cities, only Plymouth (the largest by some way, in terms of population) has anything of the urban about it. Around half the size, the university town of Exeter can by no means be considered small, but the cobbled alleyways and period town houses of its centre give it an historical ambience that is not overwhelmed by the more modern developments of the periphery. And tiny Truro, with fewer inhabitants than a typical small town, feels even more laid-back.

Part of the reason for this is undoubtedly the wealth of older buildings and monuments that can be found throughout the counties, in both urban and rural areas. With the past

origins of their produce. This mindset is embodied at the Eden Project, the huge environmental complex that is one of Cornwall's top tourist attractions.

From hotel room entreaties as to whether you really need your towels washed every day to etiquette for the great outdoors, the visitor is frequently encouraged to respect the environment. The Countryside Code, a set of rules for visitors to rural areas, includes such prescripts as taking your litter home, keeping noise to a minimum, sticking to public paths across farmland and leaving livestock, crops and machinery alone. Locally, cycling is encouraged over car use; the Eden Project even offers cyclists and pedestrians a discount on their entry ticket.

such a strong influence, modernity is kept securely in check. The cathedrals are but the largest of a multitude of churches, in both the middle of towns and the middle of nowhere, many of which date back centuries. Georgian, Regency and Victorian town houses are an elegant presence in many of the larger resorts, a legacy of prosperous past periods. In villages and ports, their equivalent is the quaint fisherman's cottage, with its low ceilings and jaunty angles. Stately municipal buildings speak of the sway that some local towns held in Britain's seafaring heyday. Another category of structure is the mysterious monuments from prehistory: monoliths, burial mounds, bridges and ceremonial circles that hint at a forgotten world of ritual.

English villages don't come much more picturesque than the cobbles and cottages of Clovelly

History

400,000–200,000 BC	Archaeological finds suggest Devon settlers made early visits into Cornwall.
30,000 BC	A jawbone subsequently found in Torquay is the first proof of human settlement in the area.
2000 BC	The Bronze Age yields a trove of archaeological finds. Wet climate drives tribes to lowland areas.
600 BC or before	The Celts transmigrate to the region, bringing with them iron implements, and build solid hill forts.
AD 50	Romans attack Exeter, which they called Isca Dumnoniorum, and establish a stronghold there. They decline to shore up their interests in the region and the Celts continue to dominate.
Around 400	The Romans' departure is swiftly followed by the arrival of the Saxons.
476–1000	The Dark Ages give rise to much of the region's mythology and folklore.

Meanwhile, Christianity is popularised.

800–1000	The Celts and Saxons unite in defiance of the invading Vikings.
1068	William the Conqueror's besiegement of Exeter puts an end to the Anglo-Saxon state and the region is absorbed into the new Norman kingdom. The new arrivals set about building castles.
1100s–1300s	Devon's cloth industry flourishes, while Cornwall, with Norman help, rises in prominence as a tin supplier to Europe. Many fishing ports are also established in this period.
1272	The first custom duties engender a smuggling trade.
1337	Norman reorganisation results in the creation of the Duchy of Cornwall granted to the monarch's son. The first recipient is Edward III's eldest son.
1497	King Henry VII's raising of war taxes brings thousands

of protestors to London in what becomes known as the Cornish Rebellion. The protestors are defeated by the king's army and their leaders executed.

1540 Francis Drake, the first Englishman to circumnavigate the globe, is born near Tavistock.

1552 The birth of Walter Raleigh, in East Budleigh, Devon. The explorer is credited with introducing the potato and tobacco to Britain.

1588 Long-held fears of Spanish invasion are realised with the Spanish Armada, which is repelled from Plymouth.

1595 The Spanish attack Mousehole, Newlyn and Penzance.

1642–51 Civil war divides the region, which plays host to several large battles.

1716 The introduction of the beam engine boosts Cornish mining.

1803–15 The Napoleonic Wars encourage well-heeled Brits to holiday at home, kick-starting tourism.

1840s The arrival of the railway in Exeter further encourages holiday-makers.

1950s Dartmoor and Exmoor become national parks.

1952 Heavy rain causes two Exmoor rivers to burst their banks, killing over 30 people in the so-called Lynmouth Floods.

1973 Britain's EU membership and subsequent policy adoption hurts local farming and fishing.

2001 Devon farming is devastated by foot and mouth outbreak.

2004 Flash floods in Boscastle are among the worst ever in the UK.

2008 A single written form of the Cornish language is agreed upon, enabling it to be taught more extensively with EU funding.

2012 Cornwall will participate in the London Olympic Games, with Falmouth playing host to sailing events.

Culture

Combine the extraordinary panoramas, mysterious ocean and eerie moors with a dense history of mythology and it is apparent why Cornwall and Devon have played such a role in Britain's cultural heritage. From some of the grande dames of English literature and a Nobel prizewinner to the folk-inspired singer-songwriters of recent times, the southwest offers plenty to keep the culture lover engaged.

Art

Stunning scenery, superb light and, historically at least, the low cost of living have exerted a strong pull on artists. The undisputed epicentre of the region's artistic life was for many years Newlyn, an artists' colony that rose to prominence in the 1880s and 1890s. Among its big names were Pre-Raphaelite painter Thomas Cooper Gotch, portrait and genre painter Albert Chevallier Tayler, and Henry Scott Tuke, best known for his nude males. The group's work focused on the natural environment as they embraced the so-called *plein air* aesthetic, and also drew heavily on social-realist themes, with many pictures detailing the hard lives of the fishermen and their families. Much of their art is on display locally.

By the start of the 20th century, the Newlyn School had lost its prominence and was eclipsed by St Ives, whose peace and prettiness were ideal for artists. The first arrivals in 1928 were three friends: Cornish fireman and artist Alfred Wood, abstract painter Ben Nicholson and painter and opium addict Christopher Wood. They were followed a decade later by sculptors Barbara Hepworth and the Russian Naum Gabo. Despite a schism in 1948, when the abstract painters in the group separated from their figurative colleagues to form the breakaway Penwith Society of Artists, the colony is still going strong. The town received recognition for its artistic importance in 1993 with the opening of the Tate St Ives, one of just two of the gallery's branches outside London. Painting continues to flourish in the region, with workshops, art stores and local pictures adorning the walls of many a hotel and restaurant.

While Devon does not have the established colonies of its neighbour, it did produce one very famous artistic son. Sir Joshua Reynolds, the foremost portraitist and possibly the most influential English painter of the 18th

Inspiring scenery makes many parts of the peninsula an artist's paradise

century, helped found and was the first president of the Royal Academy. His efforts and talent earned him a knighthood from George III.

Cinema

The unsurpassed landscapes of Devon and Cornwall have brought film-makers to the region in droves, with dozens of pictures shot every year in the two counties. The craggy, timeless terrain has lent itself to period dramas such as Jane Austen adaptations and spooky horror films, with instalments in *The Omen* and *Dracula* series partially shot on the peninsula. Directors Michael Powell, Emeric Pressburger and Alfred Hitchcock all filmed here, the last adapting several Daphne du Maurier stories. Classic British series *Poldark*, a swashbuckling historical adventure, and regional police drama *Wycliffe* were also filmed locally. Perhaps the most bizarre stretch of the imagination is to picture pleasant Holywell Bay near Newquay transformed into a tense North Korean battlefield in the 2002 James Bond instalment *Die Another Day*.

Culture

Folklore and legends

The rich folklore of Devon and Cornwall stems largely from the Celtic era (*see pp106–7*). Thanks to their seclusion from the rest of the UK, the counties' mythology thrived, unchallenged, longer than elsewhere. The legacy is evident in the stone circles on Dartmoor, which recall the druid era, and other ancient remains. Stories abound of giants, witches, pixies, ghosts and the devil. There are also the mine spirits who were fed on pasty scraps, a ghostly pair of hairy hands forcing drivers to crash and an evil sprite who drinks the blood of naughty children.

Literature

The scenery that captivated artists and attracted film-makers has also inspired writers over the years. Devon and Cornwall's contribution to literature began early, with several passion plays emerging from the latter in the Middle Ages. The region is most closely associated with Daphne du Maurier (*see pp110–11*). But an even more prolific and famous author also had strong links with the area. Queen of crime fiction Agatha Christie was born in Torquay, Devon. Although she travelled widely in adult life, the writer maintained her link with the county, and in 1938 she purchased Greenway

Mythology and folklore have inspired much of the culture of the peninsula, such as this 'pixie cottage' in Boscastle

Estate as a holiday home, now a listed building managed by the National Trust. Christie used her birth town as the setting for several of her novels, including *And Then There Were None*.

Writers as diverse as Thomas Hardy, Virginia Woolf, D H Lawrence, John Betjeman and J K Rowling were inspired by Cornwall and set some of their work there, while Samuel Taylor Coleridge's poetry features his native Devon. Local novelist Charles Kingsley has the distinction of having had his work lend its name to a North Devon town, Westward Ho! (the only place name with an exclamation mark in it in the UK). The county also features in the poetry of Sylvia Plath and Ted Hughes, who lived there together in the 1960s before their stormy marriage broke down. The peninsula can even lay claim to a Nobel prizewinner, novelist William Golding, who was born and spent childhood holidays at his grandmother's house near Newquay.

Music

Think of one particular southwest Cornwall town, and the first thing that will come to the mind of most outsiders is the Gilbert and Sullivan libretto *The Pirates of Penzance*. Though less famous, another of the duo's comic operas, *Ruddigore*, is also set in the county. But the genre most readily associated with the region is folk music, and a rich vein of festivals and customs continues to celebrate this heritage. The Celtic influence is still manifest, and

Music plays an important part in local festivals

Cornish players in particular take part in various inter-Celtic events, as well as in the county's own such festivals.

Several contemporary singer-songwriters have picked up the folk baton, such as Devonian Seth Lakeman, many of whose songs draw heavily on local areas and history for inspiration. Other local musicians of note include Coldplay's Chris Martin, soul singer Joss Stone and rock band Muse, all from Devon. The region has also attracted a few members of the American music diaspora. Singer-songwriter Tori Amos is a long-term Cornwall resident, and in 2008 members of the Jackson Five spent the summer in Devon house-hunting, although the move did not become permanent.

Festivals and events

The region has a staggering array of festivals and events, many of which are connected to its three big draws: the great outdoors, in particular the sea, food and drink, cultural traditions and ancient customs. Because of the sheer volume, if you visit outside of the winter season (when far fewer events take place), your trip is sure to coincide with something, somewhere. The numbers make a comprehensive listing impossible, so consult local tourist boards before you go, if you're interested.

Major festivals

May

Named after the local rendering of 'hobby horse', **'Obby 'Oss** celebrates the arrival of summer with maypole dancing and a procession through town in which groups of participants style themselves as a horse. The most famous version is at Padstow, where events get under way at midnight on May Day, but Barnstaple also hosts something similar.

Though organised under the name of Cornwall's most famous writer, the remit of the **Daphne du Maurier Festival of Arts and Literature** is far wider than the author's work itself, taking in comedy, music, exhibitions, fairs and displays, talks and readings by other writers, boat trips, coach trips and tours of local gardens and churches. But fans of Lady Browning won't be disappointed: her own output also features heavily. The main action is in Fowey, where du Maurier lived, but there are events elsewhere.
www.dumaurierfestival.co.uk

June–July

Exeter Summer Festival, an extravaganza of classical, folk, jazz and world music with street entertainment and comedy, is designed to have something for all age groups. Two weeks of events are staged at various venues throughout the city.

Some of the biggest names in modern pop and rock music with the slightly surreal backdrop of the biomes makes the **Eden Sessions** an atmospheric series of gigs.
www.edenproject.com

September

Featuring some of the top chefs from the county and the country, demos, cook-offs, tastings, exhibitions and master classes, the three-day **Cornwall Food and Drink Festival**, which is held in Truro at the end of the month, is a celebration of everything culinary.
www.cornwallfoodanddrinkfestival.com

Other festivals

April

| Third week | Cornwall Spring Garden Show, different venues |
| Fourth week | Exeter Festival of Food and Drink |

May

All month	Tivvy Fest, Devon
First week	Flora Day, Helston, Cornwall
Second week	Jazz Festival, Looe, Cornwall
Third Week	Devon County Show, Exeter
Fourth week/ early June	Exmouth Festival, Devon

June

| Second week | Salcombe Festival, Devon
Royal Cornwall Show, Wadebridge, Cornwall |
| Third week | Golowan Festival, Penzance, Cornwall |

July

Mid-month	Ways With Words, Dartington, Devon
Third week	St Ives Regatta, Cornwall
Fourth week	Plymouth Regatta, Devon
July or August	Port Eliot Lit Fest, Cornwall

August

| First week | Sidmouth Folk Festival, Devon |

	Beer Regatta Week, Devon Relentless Boardmasters, Newquay, Cornwall
Second week	Falmouth Regatta Week, Cornwall
Third week	Fowey Royal Regatta, Cornwall
Fourth week	Newlyn Fish Festival, Cornwall Dartmouth Royal Regatta, Devon

September

First half	County Gig Championships, Newquay, Cornwall
Second week	Truro Music Festival, Cornwall Widecombe Fair, Devon
Second and third week	St Ives September Festival

October

| Second week | Goose Fair, Tavistock, Devon
Beer Rhythm and Blues Festival, Devon |

November

| 5 | Blazing Tar Barrels, Ottery St Mary, Devon |

December

| 24 | Tom Bawcock's Eve, Mousehole, Cornwall |

Highlights

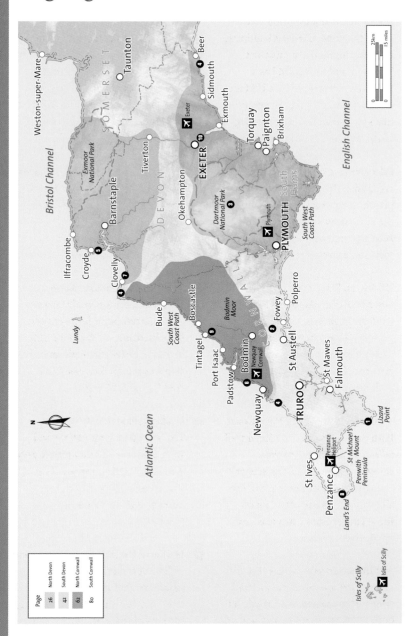

Weston-super-Mare

Taunton

Beer

Sidmouth

Exmouth

Exeter

Torquay

Paignton

Brixham

EXETER

Bristol Channel

English Channel

Exmoor National Park

Tiverton

Ilfracombe

Croyde

Clovelly

Barnstaple

Okehampton

Dartmoor National Park

Plymouth

PLYMOUTH

South Hams

South West Coast Path

Lundy

Bude

Boscastle

Bodmin Moor

Polperro

Fowey

Atlantic Ocean

South West Coast Path

Tintagel

Port Isaac

Padstow

Bodmin

Newquay Cornwall

St Austell

St Mawes

Falmouth

Newquay

TRURO

Lizard Point

St Ives

Penzance Heliport

St Michael's Mount

Penwith Peninsula

Penzance

Land's End

Isles of Scilly

Isles of Scilly

1 Cornish pasties Piping hot, easily portable and with enough energy to keep you going for a whole day down the mine, Cornwall's ultimate convenience food is a must-try. The owner of the Lizard Pasty Shop was so incensed by a US food critic's denunciation of the pasty that she burned an American flag (*see p169*).

2 Eden Project With its eco-credentials, lifelike biospheres and phenomenal volume of exhibits, the environmental complex will keep you fascinated for a day, and then some (*see pp84–5*).

3 Hiking on Dartmoor Often described as England's last great wilderness, this stunning national park will take you back in time, evoking the myth and mystery that inspired Sir Arthur Conan Doyle and others (*see pp118–19*).

4 Walking on the South West Coast Path Britain's longest national trail takes you past some of the country's most staggering scenery – and at 1,014km (630 miles) also allows you to work off some of those pasties and cream teas (*see pp40–41*).

5 Surfing at Croyde Genteel English villages are not usually associated with surfer culture, but Croyde has both excellent waves by day and an energetic post-surf scene when the sun goes down (*see pp36–7*).

6 Celebrity restaurants A Cornish culinary renaissance is being led by celebrity chefs. Jamie Oliver's Fifteen has a fantastic beachfront location, convivial atmosphere, civic motivation and, of course, great food (*see p164*).

7 Clovelly Many of Devon's villages afford a peek into bygone times, but none more so than the well-preserved and traffic-free Clovelly, the quintessential English hamlet (*see pp29–32*).

8 Land's End Windswept and wonderful, the UK mainland's westernmost point is a sight not to be missed, and its dramatic cliff views cannot fail to make an impact on even the most blasé traveller (*see pp88–9*).

9 Castles and stately homes The legend of King Arthur and splendid views give Tintagel Castle a claim to be the most exciting of the region's many impressive citadels and stately homes (*see p77*).

10 Medieval Exeter The awe-inspiring cathedral is just one of the highlights that make Exeter town centre such a delightful place for a stroll (*see pp42–9*).

Suggested itineraries

The relatively compact size of the Devon and Cornwall region – the two counties can be driven across from one side to the other in about three and a half hours – means that a lot can be packed into even a short trip, and indeed the peninsula is a popular destination for weekending Londoners and other Britons. Of course, the wealth of things to do and see will make you want to extend the visit to a fortnight or more.

Long weekend

Time pressure means that you have to be quite picky about what you see, and if you also want your weekend to be relaxing, this might mean sticking to a small area. The most famous tourist attraction is Land's End. An hour is just about enough to take in the scenery, get the picture by the celebrated signpost and do one of the theme park experiences, although it's quite possible to spend longer here on a more relaxed schedule. In the same area, the open-air Minack Theatre is an extraordinary dramatic venue, and if your trip happens to coincide with a performance, attendance is highly recommended.

The nearest main town is pretty Penzance, which is small enough for a

The Eden Project, with its focus on sustainability, is a Cornwall must-see

stroll and merits a brief stop, possibly for lunch. Close by, Falmouth and Truro are picturesque enough and have sufficient sights to take up a morning or afternoon, with Truro just shading it if you have to choose. St Ives is also recommended, particularly if you're an art lover, with several superb venues topped off by the local branch of the Tate Gallery. The town's wide range of accommodation makes this a good place to base yourself throughout your stay. It's not right on your doorstep, but you really shouldn't miss Jamie Oliver's restaurant Fifteen. Close to Newquay, it has a fantastic view of the beach and serves up some of the best food on the peninsula. It's popular, so booking ahead is advisable.

The drawback of this itinerary is the omission of Devon. If you're coming by car, however, the A30 skirts the north rim of Devon's Dartmoor National Park, affording you the opportunity of a quick stop to admire the magnificent scenery. An alternative is to take a slight detour onto the B3212, which goes right through the middle of the park.

One week

A week allows you to see all of the above at somewhat less of a breakneck speed. You can also factor in a few extra attractions. Top of the list should be the Eden Project, the spectacular environmental complex that consists of two huge biomes simulating different climates. You need two or three hours minimum here; eco-enthusiasts could

Land's End's much-photographed iconic signpost

quite happily spend the whole day and still not be ready to leave. On your way to Fifteen, you can spend a little time in surfer's hangout Newquay.

The extra few days also enable you to include Devon. Rather than simply driving through Dartmoor, you can stop for a spot of hiking or horse riding. The county's other main draw is Exeter, a beautiful university city whose imposing cathedral is its chief highlight. With a week, you can also make the effort to experience some of the region's nightlife. Pick up a listings guide and select a play or concert at one of the region's excellent large

Clovelly's donkeys are a Devon highlight

venues, or go for something more local. Falmouth, St Ives and Exeter are some of the best places for a low-key jazz night or small gig.

Two weeks

This sort of time frame allows you to take things a lot more leisurely and start spending longer in each place, wandering and discovering some of the hidden aspects and quirkier attractions rather than just ticking off the main tourist draws. You're also more likely to feel inclined to try some of the activities on offer, be it hiking for a day (or days) on Dartmoor, Exmoor or a section of the South West Coast Path, doing some of the National Cycle Network or catching some waves on the north coast.

On a two-week trip, outside of the winter months at least, you're likely to want to visit the Isles of Scilly. Though tempting, the hassle and expense of getting there can render them unappealing on a shorter holiday. With two weeks up your sleeve, you'll have the time to stay overnight, and the isolation, tranquillity and splendour (you will quite understand why the archipelago was designated an Area of Outstanding Natural Beauty by the British government) make it worth doing so. Other stops that can be added to your itinerary include the Lizard Peninsula, delightful Fowey, the traditional fishing village of Clovelly, and Torquay and its surrounds on the south coast of Devon.

Over the course of a fortnight, you're bound to find a festival or event going on in the vicinity of your planned route (unless you're travelling in winter, when the festival calendar goes rather quiet). You'll have enough time to devote a day to whatever it happens to be; these occasions often give a wonderful flavour of the region and can be great fun to boot.

Longer

Now the region really is your oyster, and your main problem will be selecting a route that takes you everywhere you want to go with the most efficiency. With so much time at your disposal, you can travel unhurriedly along the coast, entering at Exeter and then following the shoreline westwards. Of course, there is more to Devon and Cornwall than their coast. The three great untouched terrains of Dartmoor National Park, Exmoor National Park and Bodmin Moor all deserve inland detours (although Exmoor does border the sea), and you can spend extended time hiking or cycling should that be your cup of tea. Even if it's not, a stay of a few days in a remote national park village can be wonderfully rejuvenating.

This coastal route (insofar as it is possible – sometimes the road will take you a little inland) with a few choice diversions will encompass all the highlights. Your relaxed schedule will also allow you to pick and choose any festivals you might be interested in and devote a good few days to experiencing them. You can end your trip heading out of Devon through Dunster on the A39, to get back onto the M5, or picking up a bus or train connection from Exeter.

On a longer tour, you have time to take in Devon towns such as Brixham

North Devon

More off the beaten track than any other part of the peninsula, North Devon has some of the most inspiring scenery throughout the counties – and the rugged seascapes and wild rocky outcrops are all the more enjoyable for not being as overrun with tourists. With the biggest town in the area, Barnstaple, having a population of around 25,000, the lack of a bustling metropolis of the likes of Exeter adds to the sleepy feel.

Many of the larger towns have more than a hint of Victoriana about them, and the leftover porticos, pannier markets and promenades all evoke the spirit of progress and industrial advancement of that era. The comparison with today's quiet towns and the slightly greater presence of pensioners add to the general somnolence. In between the metropolitan areas, the villages continue the theme. Names such as Frithelstock, Bratton Fleming and Petrockstowe speak of a remote and bucolic corner of England, and the area is also home to the only town in England whose name includes an exclamation mark, Westward Ho!, named after Charles Kingsley's novel.

The village atmosphere has been deliberately preserved in Clovelly, a former fishing town that has been closed off to traffic and turned into a tourist attraction, but with the former residents staying on. If this smacks of too much artifice for your taste, plenty of other small stop-offs will give you a more authentic flavour – albeit with fewer things to do.

Into this sedate mix of faded Victorian towns and genteel English villages that could have easily served as inspiration for Agatha Christie's quaint St Mary Mead has come an unlikely interloper: surfing. The north coast of the peninsula has some of the best waves in both the region and the country, and mannerly pensioners now share their space with the chilled-out dudes of the surfing set.

Barnstaple

Reputedly the oldest borough in the UK, Barnstaple even gets a reference in Shakespeare, albeit under its former, probably Roman, name of Barum. The town was established at the River Taw's lowest crossing point, and the river provides a pleasing presence, skirting the town centre. Though its strategic importance – its port contributed five ships to the effort against the Spanish

Armada in 1588 – has long since diminished, it remains the main retail area for North Devon. As such, it has seen new developments and regeneration work, and lacks the sense of faded glory common to some of the other Victorian enclaves on the coast.

Although the tourist attractions proper are few, limited really to a couple of museum-type places and a church, Barnstaple is an agreeable place to spend an afternoon, particularly when the sun shines. Part of its charm is floral: the town has won the Britain in Bloom horticultural competition against towns in its population category on several occasions over the last decade or so, and you certainly get the impression of a place that wants to

make the most of what it's got. There is a very helpful **Tourist Information Centre** in the same building as the Museum of Barnstaple and North Devon (*Tel: (01271) 375000. Open: Mon–Sat 9.30am–5pm. Closed: Sun). 63km (39 miles) northwest of Exeter.*

Barnstaple Heritage Centre
Housed in a former merchants' exchange, the amiable Barnstaple Heritage Centre details the development of the town from its Saxon origins to more recent history. Mock-ups (such as one of a civil war trench) and models (a ship's cargo hold) join more contemporary and interactive exhibits such as computer

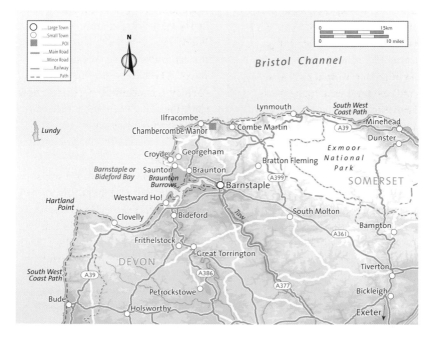

touch screens and videos (deliberately employing local people for that authentic West Country burr) in telling the Barnstaple story.

Queen Anne's Walk, The Strand. Tel: (01271) 373003. www.barnstaple-history.co.uk. Open: Apr–Oct Tue–Sat 10am–5pm; Nov–Mar Tue–Fri 10am–4.30pm, Sat 10am–3.30pm. Closed: Sun & Mon. Admission charge.

Butchers Row

Built along with the Pannier Market in 1855, the 33 shops of Butchers Row showcased superior Victorian design:

Barnstaple lays claim to being the UK's oldest borough

north-facing, to protect their wares from the heat, and with wrought-iron supports and overhanging roof. Today the name might be something of a misnomer, as just two of the businesses in the row continue to vend meat. The produce theme continues, though: newcomer shops include a bakery, delicatessen, fishmonger, florist and greengrocery.

Next to the Pannier Market.

Museum of Barnstaple and North Devon

The impressive scope of this place, housed in a former home built in 1872, should be able to answer most of the questions you have about North Devon; if it can't, the helpful staff certainly will. A series of rooms on two levels includes ecological exhibits (featuring the big animal bones that children love), plenty of Victoriana, plus a room dedicated to Barum ware, traditional red-clay pottery from the region. Even seasoned travellers who have traipsed around numerous rooms of pottery in their time will enjoy the quirky designs, which include crocodiles and sundry fish. The war section, '200 Years in Defence of Devon', has uniforms and exhibits accompanied by a wealth of captions with interesting stories and information. Huge folders with more detail are also on hand for war buffs.

The Square. Tel: (01271) 346747. www.devonmuseums.net/barnstaple. Open: Mon–Sat 9.30am–5pm. Closed: Sun. Free admission.

Pannier Market

The region's main emporium since Saxon times, Barnstaple's Pannier Market has spawned copies across the north coast of the county. Local tourist boards are proud to trumpet that the *Independent* newspaper rated it as one of the top ten food markets in the UK. The main market day is Friday and different days cater to specific wares: Tuesday, Friday and Saturday (plus Monday from April to December) is a general market with fresh food from the local area, Wednesday is for antiques and Thursday is for crafts.
High Street. Tel: (01271) 379084. www.barnstaplepanniermarket.co.uk. Open: Apr–Dec Mon–Sat 9am–4pm; Jan–Mar Tue–Sat 9am–4pm.

Parish Church

The churchyard includes the 14th-century St Anne's Chapel, former grammar school and alma mater of English dramatist John Gay, who produced *The Beggar's Opera*. It's open to the public only through a guided tour, which can be arranged via the tourist office. The main church, an imposing stone building replete with tower and steeple, is easier to visit.
Church Lane. Tel: (01271) 344589. www.barnstapleparishchurch.co.uk. Open: Mon–Fri 10am–3.30pm.

Clovelly

It's certainly possible to find fault with Clovelly. It's inauthentic, touristy,

The Widower and similar local pottery can be seen at the Museum of Barnstaple and North Devon

expensive, and its steep hill is wearing for the able-bodied, practically impassable for anyone else. But its imperfections pale in comparison to the incredible beauty and charm of the place. When you're picturing a generic, beautiful English village, it will be pretty close to Clovelly: car free, hilly, with cobbled streets almost overarched by quaint cottages and greenery, leading, of course, down to the sea.

The town's aesthetics are due to its unusual ownership situation as one of only about a dozen privately owned villages in the UK. It manages to be both tourist attraction – with a large

The privately owned village of Clovelly serves as a charming reminder of times past

visitors' centre, admission fee and usual amenities (gift shops, public toilets, etc.) – and real town. A former fishing village, the vast majority of its houses – some of which are 500 years old – are occupied by residents, many of whom suffer with good grace the repeated knocks on their door from unwitting tourists (at least, according to the official video).

The action centres on a steep cobbled path leading from the visitors' centre to the sea, where, in summer, you can depart on a boat trip. Difficult enough on the way down, it's exhausting when you come back up. (If the thought of the ascent is too much, a Land Rover service ferries visitors from the Red Lion pub up to the visitors' centre by an alternative route, between Easter and the end of October, for a charge.) The absence of vehicles means that goods have to be delivered to the village's businesses by sledges, which is quite an unusual scene. Although, as a 'real' town, the village is open to residents 24 hours a day, it has specific business hours. While you could avoid the fee by coming outside of these times, the stunning views of the Bristol Channel and exquisite cottages really merit a daytime visit, which means forking out for a ticket.

Although there are specific attractions within the village, the main pleasure is simply strolling (unless you're of an athletic bent, the gradient and ground surface prevent anything faster), absorbing the atmosphere and admiring the views. Some of the more tourist-oriented businesses and features can be safely bypassed; the more worthwhile ones are listed below. It's possible to stay overnight in the village in one of the two hotels.
26km (16 miles) along the A39, to the west of Barnstaple. Open: summer holidays 9am–6.15pm; summer 9.30am–5.30pm; winter 10am–4pm.

Clovelly donkeys
Some of the most delightful Clovelly residents are the donkeys, which can be seen walking up and down, hanging around by the side of the cobbled path for photos or a quick pet or relaxing by their stables. Since the 1990s, the animals have been mostly relieved of their erstwhile duties as beasts of burden, passing on the heavy lifting and transporting work to the human-drawn sledges. The main carrying they do these days is in the form of

giving rides to children in summer. Their keepers are happy to answer any equine-related questions you might have.
www.clovellydonkeys.co.uk

Fisherman's Cottage
Furnished in the style in which it would have been in 1936, the year Betty Asquith, daughter-in-law of the British prime minister, inherited the village, this cottage is part mock-up home and part museum. Fishing paraphernalia bedecks the walls, along with information about various shipwrecks. The property is sometimes used for demonstrations. Tall people should be wary of the low ceilings.
Open: 9.30 or 9.45am–5 or 6pm, depending on the season.

Kingsley Museum
Again, part museum and part mock-up, this shrine to Clovelly's most famous resident features information about and photos of novelist Charles Kingsley. Had it not been for the 19th-century social reformer, the village may have lain undiscovered. But his novel *Westward Ho!*, written in and heavily drawing on the village, brought it to wider attention. Kingsley's description – 'Suddenly a hot gleam of sunlight fell upon the white cottages, with their grey steaming roofs and little scraps of garden courtyard, and lighting up the wings of the gorgeous butterflies which fluttered from the woodland down to

the garden' – conveys how little the place has changed. The animatronic writer in his study may be a little kitsch for some tastes, but overall the museum is worth a visit, not least for the splendid views that make it easy to see where Kingsley got the inspiration for his classic fairy tale *The Water-Babies*. *Open: 9.30am–6pm.*

Pottery workshop

It's possible to act out your favourite scene from *Ghost* here in this working showroom, or simply buy some clay souvenirs.
Open: summer Mon–Sat 10.30am–5.30pm, Sun 11am–5pm; winter hours vary.

Visitors' centre

While some visitors might judge that the large, professional visitors' centre heralds the entrance to the quaint village itself rather incongruously, it's a useful resource for anyone interested in learning more about the background of Clovelly. A 20-minute film touches on the history of the village, including interviews with current residents and a plug for the local lifeboat service (a common feature of many tourist-attraction films in the area). There's also a shop and a large café, which sometimes stages evening events on summer weekends. *Tel: (01237) 431781. Email: visitorcentre@clovelly.co.uk. www.clovelly.co.uk. Open: summer 9am–6.30pm; winter 10am–3.30pm. Admission charge.*

Ilfracombe

It's certainly not the most chic of the region's resorts, but Ilfracombe is

Attractions such as the Fisherman's Cottage afford a glimpse of a bygone way of life

Even the more built-up coastal areas, such as Ilfracombe, are easy on the eye

North Devon's most visited one. Another of the Victorian-era towns, the place has suffered more than some of its contemporaries with the passing of time, and is popular largely among elderly visitors and families out for a no-frills seaside holiday. However, the seemingly incongruous presence of a Damien Hirst co-owned restaurant, displaying some of the artist's own works, and a nascent surfing culture are now bringing a touch of cool to this faded resort.

Despite its resolute lack of pretension and commercialisation, Ilfracombe makes a decent stop if you're in the area. The pleasant town centre has a slow pace of life, at least out of season, and the harbour is pretty enough. For somewhere of its size, there is a surprising number of interesting places to visit.

15.5km (9½ miles) north of Barnstaple.

Chambercombe Manor

It may be charming from the outside, but the pretty, whitewashed exterior belies a gruesome past. Lovers of history and the supernatural will enjoy a visit to this 11th-century Norman manor house, close to the town, mention of which was made in the Domesday Book. Chief among the draws is its reputation as one of the UK's most haunted houses (*see box, p35*). Another claim to fame is that Lady Jane Grey (famous for having the shortest reign of all English monarchs, earning her the appellation of the Nine Days Queen), whose family once owned the property, is supposed to have spent one night here; a room has duly been named in honour of the occasion. Visitors can see eight period rooms, with furnishings from the Elizabethan to the Victorian periods, and the splendid gardens and woods make a cheerful counterpoint to the manor's grisly history. Hour-long guided tours are available throughout the day.

Chambercombe Lane, off the A399 to Combe Martin, a short walk from the harbour and coast path. Tel: (01271) 862624. www.chambercombemanor.org.uk.

Open: Easter–Oct Mon–Fri 10.30am–3.30pm, Sun noon–3.30pm, Jul & Aug Sat & Sun noon–4pm, closed Sat outside high season except bank holiday weekends; closing time denotes last tour. Admission charge.

Emmanuel Church

Although the church itself is not open to visitors outside service hours, next door in the summer there is an exhibition of work by local artists.

Wilder Road (entrance on Avenue Road). Tel: (01271) 862175. Open: Easter–Oct from 10am. Free admission.

Gorgeous greens and brilliant blues make Devon one of England's prettiest counties

THE LEGEND OF CHAMBERCOMBE MANOR

In 1865, the manor's owner was fixing the roof, when he realised that part of the property had been blocked off. Smashing through the wall, he came upon a four-poster bed on which lay a woman's skeleton. Legend has it that it was the body of Kate Oatway. Kate's grandfather, who lived in the house in the 18th century, had been a notorious 'wrecker', deliberately luring ships to their demise upon the rocks to loot their valuables. Her father, William, did not follow in his brutal footsteps. He wed a Spanish woman whom he had saved from one of his father's wrecks, and led a decent life, hoping to save enough money to buy back his childhood home. The couple's daughter married an Irish captain and moved away, promising to return to visit. One night, a storm left a young woman injured on the rocks. William brought her into the house to try to save her, but to no avail. While searching her for some kind of identification, the couple found an abundance of money and jewels, which they stole. William later learned the body was that of his daughter, Kate, and, in his guilt and shame, bricked up the room.

Ilfracombe Aquarium

Water-dwellers from every kind of habitat.
The Old Lifeboat House, The Pier. Tel: (01271) 864533. Email: info@ilfracombeaquarium.co.uk. www.ilfracombeaquarium.co.uk. Open: Feb half-term–Easter 10am–3.30pm; Easter–Jun & Sept–Oct 10am–4.30pm; Jul–Aug 10am–5.30pm; Nov–Jan 10am–varies. Admission charge.

Ilfracombe Museum

Containing an almost unfathomable array of items, from snakes, skulls and soaps to old televisions, gas masks, stuffed animals, Raj memorabilia and photos of George Formby, this eclectic collection is a real labour of love. Top of the bill is a cupboard full of creepy preserved bats in jars from the 1930s.
Wilder Road. Tel: (01271) 863541. Open: Easter–Oct daily 10am–5pm; Nov–Mar Tue–Fri 10am–1pm. Admission charge.

Tunnels Beaches

Hand-carved tunnels, courtesy of Welsh miners in the 1820s, lead the way to a Victorian tidal bathing pool (check the tide times if you're going there especially) and sheltered beaches.

The eclectic exhibits of Ilfracombe Museum

Thatched roofs, whitewashed walls and small doorways – Croyde is how English villages ought to look

Bath Place. Tel: (01271) 879123. Email: info@tunnelsbeaches.co.uk. www.tunnelsbeaches.co.uk. Open: Easter holidays–Sept 10am–6pm; summer holidays 10am–7pm; Oct Tue–Thur, Sat & Sun 10am–5pm; closed Nov–Easter holidays. Admission charge.

Walker's Chocolate Emporium

Devon's answer to Willy Wonka's chocolate factory is this shop-cum-museum-cum-workshop, where chocophiles can choose from 12 different kinds of hot chocolate and a glut of other products for the sweet-toothed. *6 High Street. Tel: (01271) 867193. www.chocolate-emporium.co.uk.*

Open: Mon–Sat 9am–5pm. Closed Sun. Free admission.

Croyde

Almost impossibly picturesque, Croyde is exactly how the quintessential English village ought to look, full of tiny cottages, thatched roofs, and ponies clip-clopping through town. The pretty stream that meanders by merely adds to the postcard perfection. The place is peopled by civilised folk, many of them elderly, giving it a genteel air: it's immediately clear that this is the kind of mannered outpost where drivers are courteous and every 'give way' is accompanied by a pleasant exchange of 'thank you' waves.

It's now also a big surfer destination, and sums up the paradox of North Devon: a tiny rural post office with elderly Devonians queuing for their pensions might sit side by side with a funky surf shop where tanned, blonde dudes are waxing their boards and chatting in impenetrable jargon. Surfers love Croyde for both its waves and its charm, and it has a great reputation among the wet-suited fraternity. Despite its growth as a surfing hotspot, however, the beach has retained an untouched feel thanks in part to its grassy sand dunes.

Unless you're catching the waves, there is little to actually do in the village, but its prettiness merits a drive through or stroll. There's a few pubs, some of which can get rather lively as they cater to the surf crowd, and you can also get a traditional Devon cream tea. The surrounding villages – Georgeham, Saunton and Braunton – are also worth a look, the last in particular for the Braunton Burrows, one of the top dune systems in the northern hemisphere and part of a UNESCO Biosphere Reserve.
13km (8 miles) northwest of Barnstaple.

Tiverton

Lying in the southern part of Exmoor, this textile town's main point of interest is **Tiverton Castle**. Constructed in 1106, at the behest of Henry I, it was rebuilt and extended in the 13th and 14th centuries, and has been home to various nobles over the years. Its only

action came during the English Civil War, when New Model Army General Sir Thomas Fairfax's men fortuitously hit a drawbridge chain, and the castle fell to the attackers in 1645. Since then it has been in private hands. It is now possible to visit, but the opening hours are limited. The large church next door is also visually impressive and in keeping with the castle.
Park Hill. Tel: (01884) 253200.
www.tivertoncastle.com.
Open: Easter Sun–end of Oct Sun, Thur & bank holidays 2.30–5.30pm.
Admission charge.
21km (13 miles) due north of Exeter.

St Peter's Church, located next to Tiverton Castle, is an atmospheric presence in the town

How surfing reached the peninsula

It's difficult to conceive of surfing as a sport with much of a history – its slang terms and branded clothing lines seem to belong to the present, not the past. But it is believed that man first took to the board 3,000 years ago, as a way to fish more effectively. The activity first became known to Europeans when English explorer Captain James Cook pitched up in Hawaii in 1778, on his third expedition to the Pacific.

Cook met his death at the hands of the Hawaiians, and his successor completed his journals, including two pages on an activity practised by the locals at Kealakekua Bay, on the Kona coast of the Big Island. The first recorded account of surfing ran thus: 'The Men sometimes 20 or 30 go without the Swell of the Surf, & lay themselves flat upon an oval piece of plan about their Size and breadth, they keep their legs close on top of it, & their Arms are us'd to guide the plank, they wait the time of the greatest Swell that sets on Shore, & altogether push forward with their Arms to keep on its top, it sends them in with a most astonishing Velocity, & the great art is to guide the plan so as always to keep it in a proper direction on the top of the Swell, & as it alters its direct.'

By the 19th century, the Hawaiians had exported the sport to California, and it went global after islander Duke Kahanamoku won Olympic gold swimming medals in 1912 and 1920. He subsequently toured the USA and Australia, incorporating surfing into his exhibitions, and for three decades the sport grew steadily. It was not until the 1950s and 1960s that, helped by the Beach Boys and their idyllic depictions of the laid-back, sun-kissed surfer vibe, surfing really came to the fore.

From the South Pacific to the southwest: the surfboard has a 3,000-year history

A surfer rides a wave at Newquay

Meanwhile, in the UK, the sport had made its way to Cornwall and the Channel Islands, places where the waves were big enough, albeit with a lower profile. A rise in drownings on Atlantic Ocean beaches saw lifeguards being employed, many of whom hailed from Australia or South Africa and brought their boards with them. This inspired local watersports enthusiasts to follow suit.

On the southwest peninsula, the sport was spurred on by the local craftsmen willing to make the boards. In 1962, a group of surfers in Newquay began using the new fibreglass Malibu surfboards, and over the course of the decade Cornwall eclipsed Jersey as the epicentre of UK surf culture. From the starting point of Newquay, surfing spread along the north coast. Four decades after the sport's tentative beginnings, the region is now home to several surfing competitions, including the English National Surfing Championships, British National Surfing Championships and Relentless Boardmasters.

Cook's successor could well have predicted its popularity. He concluded his description of the Hawaiian surfers with the observation: 'The above diversion is only intended as an amusement, not a tryal of skill, & in a gentle swell that sets on must I conceive be very pleasant, at least they seem to feel a great pleasure in the motion which this Exercise gives.'

Walk: South West Coast Path

With a phenomenal 1,014km (630 miles) of seaside trail, the South West Coast Path offers an infinite number of walks, from kilometre-long meanders to the boot-busting entirety of the route. The official website (www. southwestcoastpath.com) is hugely useful, offering pre-planned walks, and a facility to help you plan your own.

The total distance of the walk is 6.5km (4 miles), and it will take you two to three hours.

Start out at Hartland Quay, a former smuggler's port about 10km (6 miles) west of Clovelly. From the car park of the Hartland Quay Hotel, look for signs to Spekes Mill and follow the path. To your right lie stunning rock formations and reefs at low tide. In a few minutes you'll reach St Catherine's Tor.

1 St Catherine's Tor

It has long since been lost to the sea, but the hill is believed to have once been home to a Roman villa or chapel. A waterfall goes down to the beach below.

Cross the stream using the stepping stones, pass through the field (following the acorn sign) and exit through the gate. Continue south along the path, which will descend rapidly, for about 1.5km (1 mile).

2 Spekes Mill Mouth

A surfing beach, the lack of road access and absence of amenities here keep Spekes Mill Mouth for the dedicated surfing cognoscenti, while submerged wrecks and rocks make it unsuitable for outsiders. To get to the beach, take the steep set of steps. Two streams intertwining for around 50m (164ft) along a fault line in the rock make this a superb series of waterfalls.

Leave the South West Coast Path and head inland on the stony public footpath, signposted Lymebridge. Go right at the fork, which will take you through a small wood. When you reach the road, turn right for Docton Mill Gardens.

3 Docton Mill Gardens

These charming gardens bloom with narcissi, primroses, camellias, rhododendrons, azaleas, bluebells and roses, depending on the time of year. If you need a rest, you can also stop here for a Devon cream tea.
Tel: (01237) 441369.
www.doctonmill.co.uk. Open: Mar–Oct 10am–6pm. Free admission.
Retrace your steps until you reach the spot where you emerged from the woods and met the road. This time,

take the opposite direction until you come to a crossroads and then go left up the hill. At Kernstone Cross, keep going straight on the farm track to Wargery Farm. Continue left on the track, which affords you excellent views of Lundy Island and the church tower to which you are headed. As it continues through some woodland, the path gets steeper and less even. Follow it until you reach Stoke. Take the road going left, signposted Hartland Quay. You'll soon reach the church.

4 St Nectan's Church

This 14th-century church, known as the 'Cathedral of North Devon', has the county's tallest church tower. The impressive 39m (128ft) structure served to guide seafarers before the Hartland lighthouse existed. Inside you'll see its original rood screen and Norman font.

From the church, take either the steps leading from the far corner to the public footpath, or the road back up to the coast path and car park where you started.

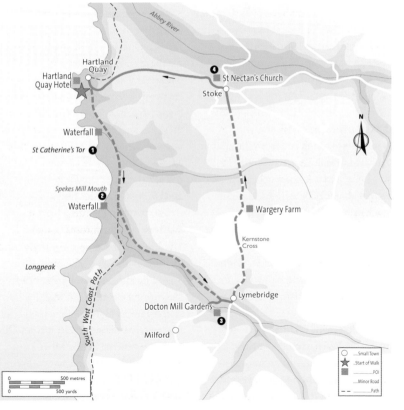

South Devon

Home to the so-called English Riviera, South Devon is diverse and attractive, with two large metropolises, a variety of appealing coastal resorts and the bucolic charm of the inland countryside. The array of places comes in a relatively compact area: from Beer, the easternmost resort covered here, to Plymouth, from where the Tamar Suspension Bridge whisks you over the river to Cornwall, is 100km (over 60 miles) and less than two hours' drive.

Though Plymouth is the larger city in the county by population, it is Exeter that is the administrative capital, and the more appealing of the two. Both offer the visitor plenty of history, activities and entertainment. The cultural scene is lively in both towns, thanks in part to Plymouth's flagship theatre and Exeter's large student population, which lends the city a laid-back vibrancy.

Just a few kilometres from these large urban centres, it's a totally different scene. The coast is home to the conurbation of Torbay, which includes the town that John Cleese's *Fawlty Towers* has indelibly established as the quintessence of English seaside resorts, Torquay. The South Devon coastline caters to every kind of holidaymaker: genteel types (often of advancing years) seeking quaint, olde-worlde resorts and Georgian and Regency grandeur, bucket-n-spaders and the back-to-nature brigade. The easternmost resorts, lying as they do slightly to the extreme end of the main strip of Devon and Cornish coastline, manage to avoid the crowds of more central places.

But the wonderful scenery is not limited to the coastline. The South Hams, which border Dartmoor to the north, represent the English countryside at its best, all unspoilt rolling hills, enchanting villages and fields of gambolling lambs. Many of these fields are part of the organic vanguard that Devon is leading, and wherever you go in this part of the county, the place exudes healthfulness and wholesomeness.

Exeter

The Romans' most southwesterly fortified settlement, Exeter is also one of the oldest towns in the UK. Unsurprisingly, then, it's teeming with history. But rather than having the staid ambience of some cathedral cities, the tradition is offset by the town's university, which results in an energy and thriving cultural life. Its centrality to Devon life – both geographically, as the end of the M5 motorway, and commercially – is another aspect that has stopped it from receding into the past, as is the case with other historical points in the region.

Small enough to explore easily on foot, Exeter is dominated by its majestic cathedral, an extraordinary feat of architecture and inescapable urban presence. The building is complemented by the old-fashioned style of its surroundings: small cobbled alleyways wind between medieval and Georgian edifices, which once housed the upwardly mobile merchants who rode on the coat-tails of the town's success. Now and again there's a snatch of the Roman city wall. But drift a little further from the centre and you're confronted with stark modernity, in the form of the spanking-new Princesshay shopping centre and the pedestrianised area around it.

57km (35 miles) northeast of Plymouth.

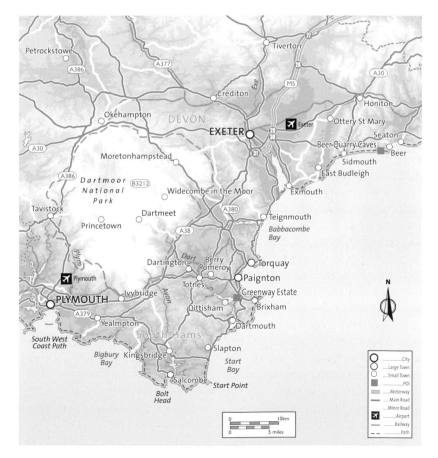

South Devon

Bill Douglas Centre

A museum and research centre for the history of cinema and popular culture, the centre is home to one of the largest such collections in the UK, many of the exhibits being donations from film professionals. The history of the medium is charted, from the late 18th century to Hollywood and modern films. Items on show include early cameras and memorabilia including kitschy models of characters from *Toy Story*, *ET* and *Jaws*, an *Indiana Jones* poster and *Superman* lunchbox, as well as various film-related books.

Cinephiles will be in their element, but the camp collection will amuse most. *Old Library, Streatham Campus, Prince of Wales Road, next to the University Chapel. Tel: (01392) 724321. www.exeter.ac.uk. Open: Mon–Fri 10am–5pm. Closed: Sat, Sun, bank holidays & over Christmas. Free admission. Bus: D.*

Guildhall

Believed to be the oldest civic building still in operation in the UK, the Guildhall oozes history, from its Renaissance-era portico and

Exeter's Quay is a popular place for socialising in warm weather

granite pillars to its panelled main chamber and portraits of sundry luminaries, including royals and local lads made good.

Exeter City Council, Civic Centre, Paris Street. Tel: (01392) 665500. www.exeter.gov.uk. Open: Mon–Fri 10.30am–1pm & 2–4pm, Sat 10.30am–12.30pm. Closed: Sun. The Guildhall is often closed for official functions so it's best to phone ahead or check online or the noticeboard outside. Free admission.

The Quay

The Quay is south of the city centre, on the north bank of the River Exe. Formerly a working port, it's now been largely given over to leisure, and hosts several eating and drinking venues that are popular at night and during the summer. Though it's just a few minutes' walk from the middle of town, there's nothing remotely urban about it, with swans and ducks languorously wending their way up and down the river, and gift shops and eateries alongside. It's quite possible to enjoy this area simply for its atmosphere, but if you do want to learn more about its history, try the **Quay House Visitor Centre** (*The Quay. Tel: (01392) 271611. Email: quayhouse@exeter.gov.uk. www.exeter.gov.uk. Open: Apr–Oct 10am–5pm; Nov–Mar Sat & Sun 11am–4pm. Free admission*). In summer, the laid-back atmosphere is further enhanced with outdoor jazz on Sundays (*Jun–Sept*).

The city's medieval centre merits exploration

Rougemont Castle and Gardens

Built at the behest of William the Conqueror, the castle dates from 1068, taking its name from the local red stone used to construct it. Sadly, the best you're likely to be able to do is have a peep through the gates: the site has never been open to the public, though its purchase by a private development partnership may see this change in the future. The peaceful and photogenic gardens, on the contrary, whose entrance is to the left of the castle gate, are put to excellent use in summer with the staging of Shakespeare plays by the Northcott Theatre, and the rest of the time by strolling visitors. Dating from 1612, Northernhay Gardens (with

Gothic glory: the stunning St Peter's Cathedral is one of Devon's most impressive sights

access from High Street and Queen Street), the oldest public open space in England, border the site.
Castle Street. Tel: (01392) 265700. www.exeter.gov.uk. Gardens open: dawn–dusk. Free admission.

Royal Albert Memorial Museum

Scheduled to reopen after extensive renovations in late 2011, this well-regarded museum has comprehensive collections covering archaeology, decorative and fine art, local and natural history and world cultures.
Queen Street. Tel: (01392) 665858. www. rammuseum.org.uk. Currently closed for major refit, future hours: Mon–Sat 10am–5pm, closed Sun & bank holidays.

St Martin's Church

Medieval churches might be a common sight in the centre of Exeter, but this one, as the most complete (it avoided both the extensive Victorian refurbishment and local bombing in World War II), is worth a look-in.
Cnr Cathedral Close & Catherine Street. Open: Mon–Fri 9.30am–4.30pm, Sat 10am–5pm. Closed: Sun. Free admission.

St Peter's Cathedral

Far and away Exeter's (and possibly even Devon's) most outstanding attraction, this Anglican cathedral reached completion around 1400, although its founding dates back to 1050. No verbal description can prepare the visitor for this impressive

place of worship. As well as the longest uninterrupted vaulted ceiling and largest canopy in England, the organ, ceiling bosses (one of which depicts Thomas Becket's murder), clock and wall memorials all deserve your attention. Make sure to spend time outside, admiring the astonishingly detailed Gothic façade. The frequently ringing bells add to the arresting ambience. A sizeable green space, surrounded by Georgian buildings, perfectly offsets this Gothic tour de force.
Cathedral Close. Tel: (01392) 255573. www.exeter-cathedral.org.uk. Open: Mon–Sat 9am–4.45pm, and for services (all times approximate). Last visitor admitted 30 minutes before closing time.

Free admission but there is a suggested donation.

Underground Passages
Initially built to improve the cathedral's water supply, these well-preserved passages are now an exciting (though not for claustrophobes) tourist attraction, which can be viewed on a guided tour.
2 Paris Street. Tel: (01392) 665887. Email: underground.passages@ exeter.gov.uk. Open: Jun–Sept & school holidays Mon–Sat 9.30am–5.30pm, Sun 10.30am–4pm; Oct–May Tue–Fri 11.30am–5.30pm, Sat 9.30am–5.30pm, Sun 11.30am–4pm. Last tour departs one hour before closing time. Admission charge.

South Devon

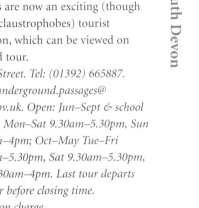
Detail of the façade of Exeter Cathedral

47

Walk: Exeter city centre

Anyone from a huge metropolis will enjoy the paradox that while Exeter has the culture and status of a big city its main attractions are all within easy walking distance. This route takes in the city's top sights, combining the medieval with the modern. For the convenience of train travellers, the route starts at the central train station.

The 3km (2 miles) can be covered in an hour, more if you want to linger at the attractions or stop for a drink.

Leave the station by the main Queen Street entrance. Go left and then left again, and you'll see Rougemont and Northernhay gardens in front of you.

1 Rougemont and Northernhay gardens

A slice of pastoral serenity in the middle of the city, these charming, well-tended gardens are great for a stroll and a sit-down (*see p45*).
Go back onto Queen Street and continue walking away from the station. After the Royal Albert Memorial Museum, the next left brings you to Gandy Street.

2 Phoenix Arts Centre

This lively centre hosts temporary exhibitions in its galleries, while the café is a bright and airy spot for lunch. *www.exeterphoenix.org.uk. Open: building: Mon–Sat 10am–11pm, Sun 11am–5pm (sometimes later for gigs or events), box office Mon–Sat 10am–8pm, Sun 11.30am–4.30pm. Free admission.*

Return to Queen Street and keep going in the same direction. Keep walking straight until you see the cathedral.

3 St Peter's Cathedral

See pp46–7.
From the front of the cathedral, any of the small lanes will take you onto the High Street and Guildhall.

4 Guildhall

In operation for over 800 years, Exeter Guildhall is believed to be the oldest civic building still in use in Britain. Its splendid Elizabethan portico gives the exterior a grandeur that is replicated on the inside, which is sometimes open to the public (*see pp44–5*).
Turn right on the High Street and continue walking. On the opposite side of the street you will soon see St Petrock's.

5 St Petrock's

One of the half-dozen medieval churches to grace the city centre, and possibly the oldest, St Petrock's is thought to have been founded by the 6th-century Cornish saint of the same name. Today, the church organisation is very involved in helping the community, in particular the homeless.

Open: Mon–Fri 9.30am–5.30pm, Sat 10am–5pm, closed Sun.

Continue walking down the High Street, which becomes Fore Street and then New Bridge Street. When you reach the river you'll see the remains of the medieval bridge.

6 Medieval bridge

Initially built towards the end of the 12th century over a waterlogged marsh, some of the original structure remains in good condition.

Walk east to the end of Commercial Road, then turn right on the quay.

7 Quayside

The city's charming quayside has shops, cafés, historical buildings and lovely river views. Round off the walk with a drink overlooking the River Exe.

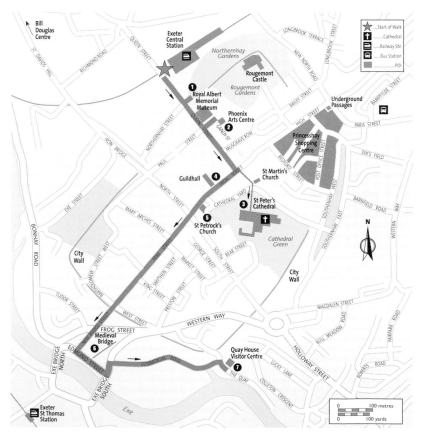

Whitewashed buildings and a balmy Mediterranean climate counteract Torquay's *Fawlty Towers* associations

Torquay

Its soubriquet, 'the English Riviera', conveys Torquay's Mediterranean pretensions, and it is true that there is a hint of that atmosphere about the place. This is largely due to the weather – the town enjoys a clement microclimate – but also to the palm trees that adorn the seafront, and the large promenade itself. But despite all this, and the whitewashed villas that climb the town's hill, this is a resolutely English resort, with pleasant greens where dogs are walked and football played, a Victorian pier and risqué seaside humour postcards. Ironically, much of the foreignness of the resort comes from an influx of visitors, both overseas tourists and English-language students.

Devon's third-largest town after Plymouth and Exeter, Torquay has more than its literary and cultural links

to recommend it. As well as providing, infamously, the inspiration for the sitcom *Fawlty Towers*, the town is also the birthplace of Agatha Christie, who

FAWLTY TOWERS

For fans of classic British comedy, it's doubtful that Torquay will ever manage to shake off its association with the inept waiting staff and manic hotel management created by John Cleese's *Fawlty Towers*, in which he starred as a snobby but hapless hotelier. The show was conceived when the Monty Python team stayed in the town's Gleneagles Hotel in 1970. The appalling service the party received and witnessed included owner Donald Sinclair criticising Terry Gilliam's 'American' table manners, mistaking Eric Idle's ticking rucksack (it had an alarm clock in it) for a bomb and hurling it over the wall, and throwing a bus timetable at a guest who enquired as to the next service. Undeterred by the atrocious depiction of the hospitality industry, subsequent owners of the hotel have proudly flagged up the connection.

drew on it for locations in several of her novels (true devotees should be able to match place and book). Two other big guns of English literature also chose the town as a base while writing their classics: Oscar Wilde's *A Woman of No Importance* and Sir Arthur Conan Doyle's *The Hound of the Baskervilles*.

There is plenty that would keep an author – or holidaymaker – here a while. Away from the main drag are quiet, elegant streets, and even the busy promenade makes a pleasant stroll. The hilly geography combined with the town's central location in Torbay affords superb views. You'll also find a lot to see (much of it Christie-related), an exciting gastronomic scene and lively nightlife.

28km (17 miles) southwest of Exeter.

Kents Cavern

This network of caves, carved into being by water movement 2 million years ago, was inhabited in the Stone Age, making it the UK's oldest dwelling place. Today it's a well-run and unusual tourist attraction. Children will love the spooky atmosphere and hearing about 'pets' of the time – which included cave bears and mammoths.

89–91 Ilsham Road. Tel: (01803) 215136. Email: caves@kents-cavern.co.uk. www.kents-cavern.co.uk. Open: Apr–Jun, Sept & Oct 9am–5pm; Jul & Aug 9am–5.30pm plus show Wed & Fri 6.30pm–late; Nov–Mar 9.30am–4.30pm. Admission charge. Bus: 32.

Torquay Pavilion is one of the landmarks with a connection to local Queen of Crime Agatha Christie

Living Coasts

Part zoo, part conservation charity, Living Coasts consists of a large aviary and several underwater viewing points. Visitors can see the animals being fed, get up close and personal to some species and listen to talks. In 2008 the venue opened its mangrove swamp habitat, the first of its kind in the country.

Torquay Harbourside, Beacon Quay. Tel: (01803) 202470, 0844 474 3366. www.livingcoasts.org.uk. Open: 10am–6pm, last entry 5pm. Admission charge.

Old Harbour

Torquay's seriously touristy bit, this is the place to come for your boat trips, souvenir shopping and promenading. *Victoria Parade.*

Torquay Museum

Devon's oldest operational museum was founded in 1844, and since then it has amassed an impressive 300,000 exhibits. Its assorted collections showcase archaeology, ethnography, palaeontology, photography, social history, oral history and ceramics. Exhibits include the testimony of wartime evacuees and a Victorian Noah's Ark mock-up, and there's an entire room dedicated to the local Queen of Crime, Agatha Christie.

529 Babbacombe Road. Tel: (01803) 293975. Email: enquiries@torquaymuseum.org. www.torquaymuseum.org.

TORQUAY'S QUEEN OF CRIME

One of the biggest publishing sensations of all time started life in a humble home on Barton Street, Torquay, in 1890. A published author at the precocious age of 11, by the time of her death in 1976 Dame Agatha Christie had written well over 100 titles, the best known of which were her 80-odd crime novels. Famously outdone only by the Bible and Shakespeare, her books have sold over a billion copies in English and another billion in translation. Though she left her childhood home at 16, the area was pivotal at many times in her life, for good and ill. Indeed, there may have been no publishing sensation had a teenage Christie not been saved from drowning at Torquay's Beacon Cove. She met her first husband at the Torquay Pavilion and honeymooned at the Grand Hotel. After extensive travels the author returned to the area in 1939, buying the Greenway estate, situated between Paignton and Dartmouth. It is now in the hands of the National Trust.

Open: mid-Jul–Sept Mon–Sat 10am–5pm, Sun 1.30–5pm; Oct–mid-Jul Mon–Sat 10am–5pm. Closed: Christmas Day, Boxing Day & New Year's Day. Admission charge.

South Hams

Delineated by the Dart and Plym estuaries, the former feudal estate of the South Hams is home to some of the finest countryside throughout the entire region. Historical relics pepper the area, and though these represent obvious draws for tourists, the towns and villages feel nowhere near as overrun as some of the resorts in the county. The eccentric village names sum up the bucolic idyll,

St Petroc's Church, at Dartmouth Castle, is set in the bucolic surroundings of the South Hams

spots like Berry Pomeroy, Buckland-Tout-Saints, Dittisham and Yealmpton. Driving around such places, it's no surprise to come across impossibly pretty scenes such as a stream ambling past a tiny, thatched cottage or a meadow of frolicking lambs.

Some of the towns are by rivers, which adds to their charm. The coastal locations, evocatively named spots such as Start Point and Bolt Head, are among the most pristine on the peninsula. The South Hams' shoreline, plus the lower Avon and Dart valleys, constitutes a significant portion of the South Devon Area of Outstanding Natural Beauty. It could be said that the shore bears more resemblance to the Mediterranean coastline than the typical English shingle beach – at least such was the thinking that saw several villages evacuated in 1944 for secret D-Day training during World War II. Main stop-offs in South Hams include Totnes, Dartmouth, Salcombe, Kingsbridge and Ivybridge. *Ivybridge is 16km (10 miles) southeast of Plymouth.*

Drive: South Hams

The stunning South Hams certainly deserves more than a drive through, but a car is a good way to see the area if you're short on time and want to pack a lot into one day.

The drive itself covers 70km (43 miles) and the walk 12km (8 miles). Allowing time to explore the towns en route and stop now and again for a drink or lunch, the trip is likely to take the best part of a day.

From wherever you are, take the A381 or 385 to Totnes. The centre is small so you can see the sights on foot.

1 Totnes

Hippy heartland Totnes was originally a Saxon settlement and has an array of striking historical buildings. A walk along the High Street will take you past the medieval East Gate, 18th-century Gothic House, Elizabethan Museum (also worth a look inside), 11th-century Guildhall and then, on Castle Street, the Norman Castle.

Drive southwest along the A381 before turning left onto the A3122 and following signs for Dartmouth.

2 Dartmouth

Since Norman times, the town has been a prosperous deepwater port, and fishing continues apace today, its pretty trawlers one of its manifold attractions. Like other South Hams towns it has a slew of ancient edifices, the oldest of all being The Cherub Pub on Higher Street,

constructed around 1380. At the bottom of Duke Street, the main thoroughfare, 17th-century Butterwalk, with its timber-framed arcade, exudes wonky charm.

Join the A379 going southwest along the coast. Behind the beach at Slapton Sands is the nature reserve.

3 Slapton Ley Nature Reserve

This 200ha (500-acre) reserve is home to all manner of birds, including the elegant great crested grebe. Access to the site is unrestricted, but guided walks are available (with a charge).

Tel: (01548) 580466. www.slnnr.org.uk. Free admission.

Continue along the A379 to Torcross and park the car. Take the coastal path down to Start Point (5.5km/3½ miles one way). If you don't want to walk, some of the way can be covered by car.

4 Start Point

Possibly the most impressive stretch of coastline in South Devon, Start Bay

runs for 16km (10 miles) from Start Point, marked by a lighthouse, to Stoke Fleming.
Return to your vehicle and continue along the A379 to Kingsbridge.

5 Kingsbridge

The epicentre of the South Hams, this town comes with the usual complement of historical buildings of note. Fore Street is the main thoroughfare, and home to Shambles market, a colonnaded structure, much of which dates from Elizabethan times.

Back in your car, take the A379 back onto the A381 to Totnes. When you reach Redworth Junction, turn left onto the A385, then join the A384 for Dartington.

6 Dartington Hall

Originally built for Richard II's half brother, this is the largest medieval house in the west of England. The highlights here include a sculpture garden and 14th-century Great Hall.
Tel: (01803) 847147.
www.dartingtonhall.com. Free admission to gardens but donation requested.

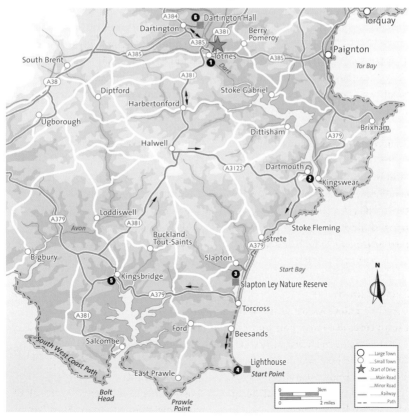

Plymouth

Though it's certainly not the prettiest of places, the heritage of Devon's largest city and a few good attractions merit half a day's exploration, while the university and optimistic urban spirit ensure a lively nightlife. Unsurprisingly, the interest lies mainly in all things maritime. It was in Plymouth that legend has navigator Sir Francis Drake (*see pp60–61*) insisting on finishing his game of bowls before confronting the Spanish Armada, and from this city that the *Mayflower* set sail, taking the Pilgrim Fathers to the New World, and thus playing a pivotal role in the history of the USA.
57km (35 miles) southwest of Exeter.

Barbican

Plymouth's old centre, west of Sutton Harbour, boasts 17th-century houses, such as **Elizabethan House** (*32 New Street. Tel: (01752) 304774. Open: Easter–Sept Tue–Sat & bank holiday Mon 10am–5pm; times vary so call ahead before making a special journey. Closed: Sun & Mon. Admission charge*).
It is also home to the **Black Friars Distillery**, brewer of the famous Plymouth Gin, which has been wetting locals' whistles since 1793 (*60 Southside Street. Tel: (01752) 665292. www.plymouthgin.com. Open: Mon–Fri 9am–5pm, Sat 11am–5pm, Sun noon–5pm. Admission charge*).

City Museum and Art Gallery

Absorbing museum with a good range of modern UK art on show, including some works from neighbouring Cornwall's two main schools of art, Newlyn and St Ives. Natural and local history are also covered.
Drake Circus. Tel: (01752) 304774.

Plymouth is chiefly known for its nautical associations

www.plymouth.gov.uk. Open: Tue–Fri 10am–5.30pm, Sat & bank holiday Mon 10am–5pm. Closed: Sun & Mon. Free admission.

National Marine Aquarium

The UK's largest aquarium also houses its deepest tank. Three floors are arranged according to habitat, with over 4,000 creatures represented and 50 live exhibits. The big draws are, of course, the sharks and sea horses, and the colourful coral is also popular. All manner of weird and wonderful water denizens dwell here; it's little wonder the managers recommend you spend three hours.

Ropewalk, Coxside. Tel: (0844) 893 7938. www.national-aquarium.co.uk. Open: Apr–Sept 10am–6pm; Oct–Mar 10am–5pm. Last admission one hour before closing. Admission charge.

Plymouth Hoe

Often windswept Plymouth Hoe, 'the Hoe' to locals, is the grassy esplanade facing out to the bay known as Plymouth (or the) Sound. Its super sea views set off several points of interest on the Hoe, including the former lighthouse **Smeaton's Tower** (*Open: summer Tue–Fri 10am–noon & 1–4.30pm, Sat & bank holiday Mon 10am–noon & 1–4pm; winter Tue–Sun & bank holiday Mon 10am–noon & 1–3pm. Last entry 30 minutes before closing. Admission charge*) and several statues and memorials of note. The well-tended grassy area has

A stained-glass window at St Andrew's Church

plenty of benches and there are a couple of cafés.

St Andrew's Church

Although the original 15th-century building was largely destroyed by a World War II bomb, this impressive reconstruction warrants a viewing. The church played a key role in city life, and the charming stewards are delighted to fill visitors in on its history (associations with Francis Drake, Captain Bligh of the *Bounty* and Francis Chichester) and point out the most interesting features. The six stained-glass windows may be barely 50 years old but they are a top draw.

Royal Parade. Tel: (01752) 661414. www.standrewschurch.org.uk. Open: Mon–Fri 9am–4pm, Sat 9am–1pm, Sun services at 8am, 9.30am, 11am & 6.30pm. Free admission.

Sidmouth once attracted high society

Sidmouth

Pleasantly posh Sidmouth, which has over 500 listed buildings, was once popular with high society, seeing a mini-influx of aristocrats in the 19th century. Today, crenellations, wrought iron and period windows hint at the town's royal heritage and continue to attract a genteel, generally older demographic. Constant attempts are still made to further beautify Sidmouth, and its floral displays have seen it take several Britain in Bloom horticultural prizes. Ascend the nearby hills, either by car or by the coast path, and you'll be met with fantastic views of the bay, as well as potential glimpses of birds that take shelter in the red cliffs.

The town's wide esplanade dates from Regency times. Away from the seafront, the regal pretensions give way to a bucolic idyll of quaint shops purveying fudge and similar village goodies. It is these pastoral traditions that lie behind the town's most important event, Sidmouth Folk Festival (*see p19*).
20km (12¹/₂ miles) east of Exeter.

Beer

Tiny, picturesque and authentic, Beer is one of Devon's treasures. Fishing remains at the core of the village, and the utterly beautiful, shingle, cliff-sandwiched beach is dotted with colourful boats and the eye-catching detritus of the industry. Sea Hill, the steep road down to the beach, has several vendors selling as fresh piscatorial wares as you can get. The bay's seclusion made it a perfect spot for smugglers. In the 18th and 19th centuries, brandy, tea, tobacco and silk

'THE ROB ROY OF THE WEST'

The swashbuckling adventures of Jack Rattenbury have made him the figurehead of Beer's smuggling fraternity. After deeming fishing too dull a career, the Beer-born boy first joined a privateer, but his verve and proficiency in hiding and escaping (from the French, excise men, prison guards and the press gang) soon drew him to smuggling. He transported conventional contraband, as well as anything else that needed shifting: he was once caught smuggling French prisoners. Despite several prison sentences – an occupational hazard – Rattenbury advanced in his career, punctuating his smuggling with legitimate enterprises such as acting as a consultant engineer to the government and running a pub. He ended his career as an author, publishing an exuberant account of his life, *Memoirs of a Smuggler*, in 1837.

made their furtive way into the inlet, to be secreted in the nearby caves, now one of the town's main tourist attractions. **Beer Quarry Caves** have been operational since Roman times. The removed stone can be seen in constructions all over the county, as well as in Westminster Abbey, St Paul's Cathedral and the Tower of London.
1.5km (1 mile) west of the village. Tel: (01297) 680282. www.beerquarrycaves.fsnet.co.uk. Open: Mon before Easter–end Sept daily 10am–5pm; Oct 11am–4pm. Admission charge. 11km (7 miles) east of Sidmouth.

Brixham

At the southern end of the Torbay conurbation, Brixham is opposite Torquay. It's a pretty, hilly town, with pastel-coloured houses overlooking the harbour, where the main action is. The focal point of the place is the life-size replica of the *Golden Hind*, Sir Francis Drake's ship. Children will enjoy exploring the deck and quarters.

Tel: (01803) 856223. www.goldenhind.co.uk. Open: Mar–Oct 10am–4pm; summer holidays 10am–7pm. Closed: winter. Admission charge. 7.5km (4^1/$_2$ miles) south of Torquay.

Exmouth

With the smell of fish and chips in the air, Exmouth is a resolutely traditional British town. Said to be Devon's oldest seaside resort, its history is evident in its seafront promenade and pleasant Georgian, Victorian and Edwardian terraces – Nelson's and Byron's wives were both fans. Offsetting this, the resort's exposed position at the estuary of the River Exe has facilitated water and wind-powered activities such as kite-surfing and windsurfing. **Exmouth Market** is a good place to pick up some excellent-value holiday gifts among other merchandise.
The Strand. Tel: (01395) 264347. Open: Aug Mon–Sat 9am–5.30pm, Sun 10am–4pm; year round Mon–Sat 9am–5.30pm. 16km (10 miles) south of Exeter.

The coves at beautiful Beer made it fertile smuggling territory

Sir Francis Drake

Sir Francis Drake certainly divides opinion. To some he was a hero, to others a pirate; to some a slave trader, to others a saviour; dragon, snake, knight... the list goes on. But what is beyond doubt is his record and reputation. The first Englishman to circumnavigate the globe (albeit not deliberately), he played a crucial role in the navy that vanquished the Spanish Armada. He remains famous for the probably apocryphal story of his sangfroid on the bowling green.

Drake was born in 1540 just south of Tavistock (where he is commemorated with a statue), the eldest of 12 brothers. He learned to sail young, and his first voyage to the New World came at 23. He was with the same fleet in 1569, when it was caught by Spaniards in Mexico, initiating an enmity against that nation that was to have far-reaching repercussions.

Drake operated as a privateer, attacking the Spanish at the instigation of Queen Elizabeth. One voyage took him to the southern tip of South America, where his ship was blown so far off course he reached the Antarctic, thereby becoming, inadvertently, the first explorer of that continent. No fellow navigator went so far south until James Cook in 1773. Returning to England, Drake continued to attack the Spanish, on both land and sea (their ships were returning from South American colonies full of riches), and arrived home laden with treasure and his surviving men in good health.

In 1579, he sailed to North America, where his chaplain held Holy Communion, one of the first Protestant church services to take place in the New World. His efficacy as a privateer was a boon to his monarch back home. The queen's half-share of one voyage's haul surpassed the crown's entire income from other sources for that year. In 1581, Queen Elizabeth knighted Drake on his ship, the *Golden Hind*, much to the wrath of the Spanish king. Drake also became Mayor of Plymouth and an MP. Though the monarch downplayed his exploits and had them declared classified, to keep the details from Spain, she and the explorer dined together and exchanged gifts.

When war erupted between Spain and England in 1585, Drake was soon off sacking Spanish ports, prompting its ruler Phillip II to order the invasion

Drake's continuing influence is evident in Brixham's replica of the *Golden Hind*

---

of England. Drake was proactive in the defence of his country, and served as vice-admiral in command of the fleet that conquered the Spanish Armada. A famous anecdote goes that while playing bowls at Plymouth Hoe in the run-up to the Battle of Gravelines, Drake was warned that the Spanish were en route. His nonchalant response was that there was plenty of time to finish the game and then defeat the Armada.

Drake continued to sail well into his 50s. A catastrophic campaign against Spanish America in 1595 saw a cannonball fired through the cabin of his flagship. Drake survived the assault, only to succumb to dysentery the next year. He was buried at sea. Before his death, the explorer ordered that the snare drum he took around the world with him be kept at Buckland Abbey in Devon. Drake vowed that were England ever in trouble, the beating of that drum would rouse him to return and defend his country.

North Cornwall

Battered by the Atlantic Ocean, North Cornwall has some of the most dramatic and rugged coastline of the peninsula. Here vast waves (often with surfers in their midst) crash down onto the sand, there craggy cliffs protrude into the sea, and further along is an unspoiled bay seemingly lifted from a 19th-century novel. Old buildings whisper of Cornwall's past, and nowhere is that past more mystical and legendary than at Tintagel, former seat of King Arthur.

This combination of enticements has not gone unheeded: the North Cornish invasion has occurred on several fronts. First there are the wet-suited dudes, making their way from all over the UK to Newquay, the self-proclaimed British surfing capital, and the other beaches in the vicinity that see the big waves. To cater for them, a whole industry has sprung up, primarily providing the obvious accoutrements such as boards, suits and lessons, but also supplying the après-surf nightlife.

The second North Cornwall invasion has been gastronomic. Celebrity chefs such as Jamie Oliver have opened restaurants in the area, thus upping the bar for local restaurateurs and raising standards across the board. This has had the effect of increasing the area's profile, and bringing in a lot of second-homers – something local people say leaves their villages like ghost towns for much of the year. In places like Padstow, the 'Rick Stein effect' is credited with having sent property prices soaring, and pricing local buyers out of the market. North Cornwall is in some ways a victim of its own success.

The politics rumbles on, but for the visitor, the fashionable eateries and the changes for which they are the catalyst are an unalloyed good. Whether it's the food or waves in Newquay and Padstow, the myths of Bodmin and Tintagel or the prettiness of just about everywhere, this part of the county more than measures up.

Newquay

Set high above the sea, the town of Newquay is the antithesis of the quaint 'Miss Marple' English village resorts elsewhere on the peninsula: big, noisy and 'in your face'. This is due, in part, to its status as unofficial surfing capital of the UK. The hordes of young surfers who come for the waves hit the town at night. But Newquay also has something of the quintessential British party town – the south coast's answer to Blackpool. At night, boisterous groups of young men and women roam the town centre, and while this may be great if you've come for the drinking and dancing, sedate and civilised it is not. The atmosphere gets exceptionally heady after teenagers finish their exams, and anyone unused to British binge culture might be rather shocked.

That's not to say that Newquay lacks the assets you'd find elsewhere on the coast. Its elevation lends the town itself marvellous views of the extended area, and the pristine coastline here is quite fabulous, backed by dramatic cliffs and grassy headlands. Jamie Oliver's restaurant in nearby Watergate Bay (a beautiful drive along the coast) has put pressure on local businesses to raise their game, and the town now hosts a decent selection of eateries. It's also a good place for a family holiday, with several attractions geared towards children. And there's plenty of greenery which makes the place easy on the eye.

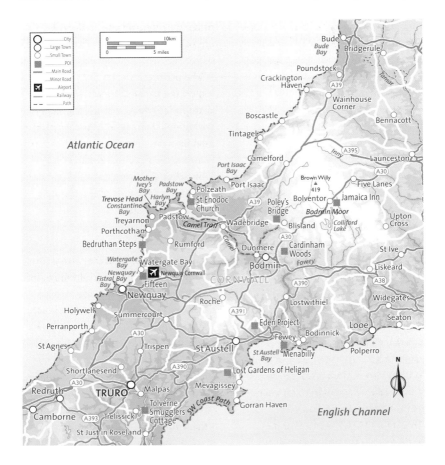

While in high season the main beaches can feel like they're packed with bumper-to-bumper windbreaks, if you're prepared to go a little outside the main drag, you'll find something resembling seclusion. Away from the slightly downmarket city centre, the rolling hills and picturesque churches are typically Cornish.

17.5km (11 miles) north of Truro.

Blue Reef Aquarium

Part of a small chain, Blue Reef has a philosophy that emphasises learning and interaction. Open-top tanks allow visitors to get up close and personal with the less vicious marine residents. Sea horses are among the most popular creatures on show, along with the

Small fishing boats dot the harbour at Newquay

octopuses, jellyfish and weird-looking rays. A shark lagoon exhibit also goes down very well with young visitors.
Towan Promenade. Tel: (01637) 878134. www.bluereefaquarium.co.uk. Open: Mar–Oct 10am–5pm; Nov–Feb 10am–4pm. Last admission one hour before closing. Admission charge.

Fistral Bay

Probably the best-known surfing beach in the country, Fistral's reliable, left-breaking waves are some of the best in the business (at least in the UK, anyway). The straight and sandy beach, which runs for about 750m (820yd), faces northwest. Backed by sand dunes, high tide shrinks the available sand quite significantly, which can rather pack it out. Exposure to swells keeps the waves consistent, and this regularity has meant several high-profile international surfing festivals have been staged here. The area is also home to the British Surfing Association (*www.britsurf.co.uk*), the sport's national governing body. Fistral is famous among the surfing community for the 'cribbar', a scarce, enormous (again, by British standards) wave generated by a shallow reef beneath the headland north of the beach. It results from a rare combination of a low spring tide with a southeast wind, which usually only occurs about once a year. The cribbar has had a lager named in its honour.
West of town. Bus: 526, 500, 588 (summer only).

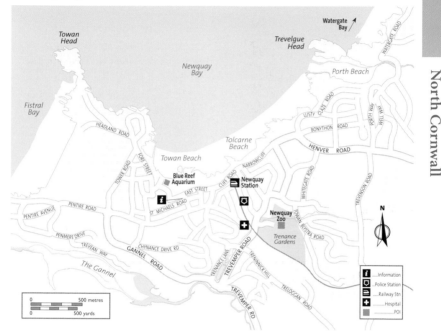

North Cornwall

Newquay Zoo

With a daily programme of events such as walks, talks and feeding, the zoo tries to make your visit an interactive experience. Aside from the animals themselves, there is plenty to entertain children, especially in summer when face-painting and other creative activities are put on. Around 300 animals are housed in over 4ha (10 acres) of land. There's also a wealth of botanical life supporting its zoological counterpart.

Trenance Gardens, off the A3075 Edgcumbe Road. Tel: (0844) 474 2244. Email: info@newquayzoo.org.uk. www.newquayzoo.org.uk. Open: Apr–Sept 9.30am–6pm; Oct–Mar 10am–5pm. Last admission one hour before closing. Admission charge.

Watergate Bay

Perhaps most famous as the site of Jamie Oliver's restaurant Fifteen (*see p164*), Watergate is also a magnet for watersports enthusiasts, owing to its northwesterly exposure. The English National Surfing Championships are held here. Large and flat, the beach makes a great backdrop to lunch.

3km (2 miles) north of Newquay on the B3276. Bus: 556, T10 (summer only).

Padstow

Tourism may now have eclipsed Padstow's traditional economic

Wild flowers at Treyarnon Bay

mainstay of fishing, but enough of the latter remains that the atmosphere and activities of a fishing village have not been entirely lost. Of course, the boom in tourism also feeds demand: Rick Stein, with his manifold establishments built up over a quarter of a century in Padstow (or Padstein, as some locals have dubbed it), must be a bulk buyer of the town's main commodity, bringing tourists from all over the UK and beyond to try everything from his highfalutin Singapore chilli crab to plain old battered cod and chips.

As well as upsetting the locals – soaring property inflation has priced them out of the housing market – the Rick Stein effect means that Padstow can get overrun in summer, particularly because of its size. But as in many popular Cornish holiday spots, if you're prepared to go a little way from the centre, there is some peace and privacy to be had.

Despite the potential crowds, you'll certainly want to check out the harbour, a hive of activity. And despite the recent gentrification, in the form of posh shops and expensive eateries, the harbour has retained much of its pre-Stein quotidian character, giving visitors a glimpse of an authentic Cornish port.

Less authentic, perhaps, but very enjoyable are the regular brass band concerts hosted, along with visiting entertainers, on the large quayside over the summer. Colourful trawlers help prettify the place, although many of the boats bobbing around the harbour are for taking tourists and second-homers out rather than reeling the day's catch in.

DOOM BAR

The appropriately named Doom Bar is a sandbank at the mouth of the River Camel, about 1.6km (1 mile) out of Padstow. Between tides, it lies just a metre or so below the surface of the sea, invisible to mariners. This treacherous obstacle is said to have claimed around 300 ships, exacting a huge toll of human lives. Livelihoods have also been hit, for the bank impeded the development of Padstow as a major commercial port. While the most likely cause is a gradual build-up of drifting sand, another, more intriguing, explanation has been suggested. One day a mermaid, who guided large vessels safely to shore, was shot by a fisherman who mistook her for a seal. Before she perished, she swore to ruin the harbour as revenge, and summoned up a huge storm which destroyed ships and created the sandbank. Like other natural features in the region, it has since given its name to a local beer.

Away from the harbour, many of the town's roads are car-free, which makes parts of Padstow amiable spots for a wander to escape the masses. Much of the place is medieval in origin, and residents' flower boxes add to the pretty English village aesthetic. The provincial scenery is augmented by some splendid beaches.
22.5km (14 miles) up the coast from Newquay.

Beaches
Though for surfers it comes second to nearby Newquay, Padstow has several beaches with decent enough waves to attract the board-n-wax crew. The best spot in the area for surfing is **Constantine Bay**, 1.5km (1 mile) south of Trevose Head, the headland 6.5km (just over 4 miles) to the west of town. Clear waters, rock pools and dunes make this spot popular, although the rocks can make swimming inadvisable. Both swimming and surfing are possible at peaceful **Harlyn Bay**, some 4km (2½ miles) west of Padstow. The wide expanse of sand at low tide, rock pools and waves make **Treyarnon**, 2.5km (1½ miles) south of Trevose Head, appealing to both surfers and non-surfers, but the local surfeit of caravan parks can flood the beach with tourists in high season. The same is true of the quaintly named **Mother Ivey's Bay**. For this reason, craggy **Porthcothan**, 1.5km (1 mile) further south, can be a better choice for solitude-seekers. Purely for their striking visual appeal, visit **Bedruthan Steps**, further south along the coast, and see rough pillars of rock said to have been the stepping stones of a mythical giant.

National Lobster Hatchery
This little-trumpeted tourist attraction is fascinating to visit and plays a critical role in underpinning the fishing industry on which Padstow's ongoing prosperity depends. An independent charity, the hatchery's remit is to rear lobsters and release them into the sea to keep the stocks up. Baby lobsters spend four to six months at the facility before their departure. As well as learning about conservation and intriguing lobster biology (they shed and eat their own skeletons and taste with their feet),

Padstow's National Lobster Hatchery

Padstow's most famous denizen is chef Rick Stein

visitors also have the opportunity to see the creatures themselves, as both newborns and adults.
South Quay. Tel: (01841) 533877. Email: info@nationallobsterhatchery.co.uk. www.nationallobsterhatchery.co.uk. Open: summer 10am–6pm; winter 10am–5pm. Times can vary. Admission charge.

Padstow Museum

Set up in 1971 by a bunch of local enthusiasts, this endearingly small amateur museum, housed entirely in one room, covers the town's history over the past two centuries. The most memorable exhibit is an 'obby 'oss from the 1940s, a model horse used in the famous festival of the same name.
1st floor, Padstow Institute, Market Place. Tel: (01841) 532752.

www.padstowmuseum.co.uk. Open: Easter–Oct Mon–Fri 10.30am–4.30pm, Sat 10.30am–1pm. At other times by special arrangement. Admission charge.

Prideaux Place

Grand Elizabethan manor house of the kind occupied by landed, murderous families in Agatha Christie novels. Indeed, the place has served as a location for various productions. The Prideaux family, whose seat this has been for more than four centuries, open it up to visitors for part of the year. Inside you'll see ornate fittings, sweeping staircases and royal portraits. There are also rumours (denied) of hauntings. The extensive grounds are undergoing restoration.
Tregirls Lane (B3276). Tel: (01841) 532411. www.prideauxplace.co.uk. House open: Easter & mid-May–early Oct Sun–Thur 1.30–4pm. Grounds and tearoom open: Easter & mid-May–early Oct Sun–Thur 12.30–5pm. Admission charge.

St Enodoc Church

On the other side of the estuary from Padstow, this 13th-century church was a favourite of poet laureate John Betjeman, who went so far as to pen the poem *Sunday Afternoon Service at St Enodoc* about it, and is buried here, on the right-hand side of the entrance gate as you enter. For three centuries, the charmingly archaic Grade I listed building was itself buried by sand from the nearby dunes, with vicar and

THE CAMEL TRAIL

Named after the river, the Camel Trail is around 29km (18 miles) of cycle route, which runs from Padstow to Poley's Bridge, close to Bodmin Moor. Largely traffic-free, part of the track follows a disused railway line, formerly the preserve of the London and South West Railway. Walkers are also welcome to follow the route, part of which (Padstow–Dunmere) is also open to horse riders. The scenery, of course, is the main attraction, and parts of the trail are also home to several avian species. Dromedaries, on the other hand, are not a common sight.

the first one. The current structure, which dates from the 15th century, uses stone from Normandy. The 14th-century font (engraved with the disciples) and wineglass pulpit are two of the more noteworthy fittings, as well as a carving of a fox sermonising to a flock of geese.

Church Street.
www.padstowparishchurch.org.uk.
Open: Apr–Sept 9am–5pm; Oct–Mar 9am–4pm. Free admission.

parishioners entering by a hole in the roof. Interesting features include a 12th-century granite font and listed tomb chests.

Rock. Open: 7.30am–dusk. Free admission.

St Petroc's Church

This large church, dedicated to the 6th-century Celtic monk, is the third to have occupied the site since he built

Bodmin

It's difficult to walk far in this heartland of Cornish pride without seeing the black and white flag of St Piran, adopted as the symbol of Cornish nationalists, flying from a pub or other property. The place has been a hotbed of revolt and mutiny, with three separate uprisings originating locally: the Cornish Rebellion of 1497, an

Prideaux Place, an Elizabethan manor house, has been a family seat for over four centuries

attempt to usurp the throne the same year, and the Prayer Book Rebellion of 1549. Bodmin was once the county town and the only Cornish settlement of significance noted in the Domesday Book. But its refusal to yield land in the 1870s to the Great Western Railway resulted in the loss of its administrative power to Truro.

A no-frills market town, Bodmin is not the most picturesque place in Cornwall. But although it might compare unfavourably with some of its neighbours, it's pretty enough by British standards, and its location to the west of Bodmin Moor (*see 'Getting away from it all', p117*) makes it a good gateway to the area. It also has a selection of gripping and unusual tourist attractions.

26km (16 miles) east of Newquay.

Bodmin Jail

Dank and gruesome, this morbidly atmospheric tourist attraction is housed in the former jail, which ceased operating as such a century ago. Before the closure, over 50 wretched miscreants were hanged here. An 'enlightened' correctional facility, it was the first prison to keep its inmates in separate cells (albeit often packed with ten fellow felons) rather than communally. The jail was also used to store the Domesday Book and the Crown Jewels during World War I. The lives of the inmates are conveyed through mannequins and stories on the wall.
Berrycoombe Road.
Tel: (01208) 76292.
www.bodminjail.org. Open: 10am–dusk.
Admission charge.

Bodmin and its surrounds are blessed with several striking historical churches, such as St Conan's in Washaway

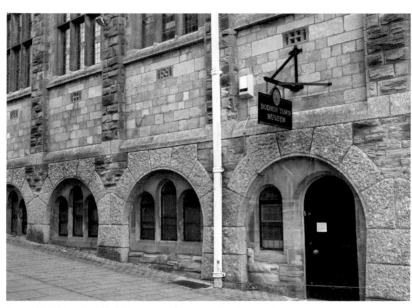

Steeped in history, Bodmin is home to various evocative sights and museums

Cardinham Woods

Beautiful mixed woodland where lucky walkers might happen upon a deer or an otter among the meandering streams.
3km (2 miles) east of Bodmin.

Courtroom Experience

Housed in 19th-century Shire Hall, formerly the county court, this appropriate attraction re-creates the real-life trial of Matthew Weeks, who was accused of murdering his former lover Charlotte Dymond on Bodmin Moor in 1844. At the time, his conviction and subsequent hanging were the subject of much doubt. After the film and waxwork-led re-enactment you get to cast your vote on his guilt or innocence. You can also visit the smelly holding cells downstairs. A tourist information office and small museum are adjacent.
Shire Hall, Mount Folly. Tel: (01208) 76616. Open: summer Mon–Sat 11am–4pm; winter Mon–Fri 11am–4pm. Admission charge.

St Petroc's Church

Cornwall's largest church dates back to the 15th century, although there has been subsequent restoration. The richly engraved Norman font, Vyvian tomb and ivory casket that once contained the bones of the saint are the highlights.
Priory Road. Tel: (01208) 73867. www.st-petroc-bodmin.co.uk. Open: Apr–Sept Mon–Sat 11am–3pm, Sun for services, other times by appointment. Free admission.

Incomers, the Rick Stein effect and Cornish nationalism

While the hospitality industry in Cornwall offers as warm a welcome as anywhere else, there are parts of the community who look upon the incursion of outsiders with a much dimmer view. Second-homers, tempted by the scenery and sunshine, have pushed up property prices to the chagrin of local would-be buyers, while some natives are going so far as to call for Cornish independence.

Resistance to the invasion has a bogeyman in the form of fish restaurateur and TV chef Rick Stein, who opened his first outlet in Padstow in 1974, which now forms part of a sizeable business empire of restaurants, shops and pubs. His eateries raised the profile of the area, pulling in well-off foodies from London and elsewhere, some of whom liked the town so much they bought homes there. While 'Padstein' undoubtedly generated much-needed revenue (Cornwall is the UK's poorest county), the increased demand for homes has seen house prices soar, with the result that young Cornwallians cannot afford to live where they grew up.

Resentment at this state of affairs has stoked a simmering nationalism, also known as the Cornish self-government movement. Proponents believe that rather than being a county in England, Cornwall is a duchy and separate state, which never officially became part of the UK. Some want it to be designated a home nation, and call for a Cornish Assembly to govern local affairs, as is the case in Wales and Scotland.

The movement is supported by a developed political infrastructure. Mebyon Kernow, founded in 1951, is the main party fighting for greater Cornish autonomy, with the Celtic League, Celtic Congress, Revived Cornish Stannary Parliament, Cornish Nationalist Party, Cornish Solidarity, An Gof and Tyr Gwyr Gweryn sharing the same objective.

Some have adopted radical tactics in their struggle. A group using the name of An Gof detonated a bomb in a St Austell courthouse in 1980, and claimed responsibility for several fires and other acts of violence throughout the decade. In 2007, the group declared it was waging a campaign against the English flag being flown in the county. The same year, another militant group, the Cornish National Liberation Army, made threats against Jamie Oliver and Rick Stein (both dubbed 'incomers'), saying it considered their customers' cars legitimate targets. A flag of St George was destroyed and 'English out' daubed on a wall. While the red cross was increasingly reviled, the Cornish flag of St Piran, a vertical white cross on a black background, grew in popularity and can now be seen hanging from proud Cornish businesses all over the county.

For now, the violence has subsided and Cornwall remains in an uneasy truce between the tourism that is its economic lifeblood and the forces fomenting local frustration. The issue does, though, occasionally erupt into the public consciousness. Support came from an unexpected quarter when, in 2004, an episode of *The Simpsons* that ran against the Queen's speech on Christmas Day featured Lisa shouting '*Rydhsys rag Kernow lemmyn*', or 'Freedom for Cornwall now' and displaying a banner with the words 'UK out of Cornwall'.

A sight to stir the heart of any proud Cornishman or woman: the flag of St Piran

Boscastle

Famous for the flash floods which submerged the town in 2004, as well as its Thomas Hardy connections, small Boscastle has the only harbour in 32km (20 miles) of coastline. Tucked into a deep hollow on the coast, its hills are dotted with thatched, whitewashed cottages, and much of the land is in the care of the National Trust.

In many respects it seems to have changed little since Hardy's day. The novelist and poet came to the town as an architect in 1870 to renovate the church of St Juilot, met his first wife Emma Gifford here and drew on the location heavily in his work, returning after Gifford's death to write poetry dedicated to her. A circular walk taking in some of the points associated with the writer can be undertaken from Fore Street or the main car park, where you'll find a map.

Hardy aside, the town's other official attraction is the **Museum of Witchcraft**. This painstakingly organised collection is tremendous fun to explore. You'll find all manner of witchy paraphernalia such as broomsticks, dunking stools, nooses, herbs, tarot cards, poppet dolls, amulets and animal skulls, as well as Harry Potter memorabilia and a spoon donated by Uri Geller. The captions detail the fascinating world of spells, magic, healing, devil worship, discrimination and hysteria surrounding the concept of the witch. The building has a stairlift.

The Harbour. Tel: (01840) 250111. Email: museumwitchcraft@aol.com. www.museumofwitchcraft.com. Open: Apr–Oct Mon–Sat 10.30am–6pm, Sun 11.30am–6pm. Last admission 5.30pm. Admission charge.

Boscastle is 41km (25¹/₂ miles) northeast along the coast from Newquay.

Bude

Though green Bude itself is pretty enough, with a 19th-century canal, central garden and fountain, it's the large beach that is its major selling point. The huge expanse of sand, often home to surfers and other wind-powered sports enthusiasts, is ruggedly scenic, and when the tide is out it is

Cecil Williamson's Crystal Ball
This crystal ball was owned and used by occultist Cecil Williamson, the founder of this museum. It was passed to the museum on his death in 1999.

A supernatural exhibit at Boscastle's fascinating Museum of Witchcraft quite a walk from the town to the water. The last resort of significance before the Devon border, Bude is surrounded by splendid cliffs, and is further prettified by the River Neet, around which it was built. Other sights include Bude Castle (although 'castle' may be rather overegging the pudding, as it's more of a compact mansion), built by the wonderfully named local inventor Goldsworthy Gurney, whose famous 'Bude light' was used in the House of Commons. The castle hosts temporary art exhibitions and has a restaurant (*www.thecastlerestaurantbude.co.uk*). *59km (37 miles) northeast along the coast from Newquay.*

Port Isaac

Occupying a rare space in the cliffs that dominate the coastline in this part of Cornwall, this isolated port has avoided the worst excesses of the tourist

Verdant and serene, Bude affords a fine family day out

THE BUDE BOOM

Quiet, quaint Bude is not ostensibly the kind of place that would be rocked by mystery explosions. But on 26 October 2006, a huge bang was heard over Bude and nearby Holsworthy, shaking residents' houses, some of which sustained damage. The 'Bude Boom', as it became known, prompted much speculation about its cause. No evidence was ever found of explosion. One theory put forward was an aircraft going supersonic too close to the ground, but the Ministry of Defence, RAF and Civil Aviation Authority all denied that any of their planes were in the area at the time. To this day, the most likely explanation remains a meteor exploding.

invasion to preserve its serenity and fishing village atmosphere. Admittedly, you may see the odd celebrity (its good looks and distance from the main tourist trail have made Port Isaac a choice location for various productions, as well as for the rich and famous seeking secluded holiday homes), but the place retains its small-town charm: scallops may be for sale on the street at an unmanned table, with customers trusted to leave the money there. Of course, the scallops, crab and lobster make for superlative meals served in the town's clutch of good eateries.

Its cragginess can lend Port Isaac a stunning panorama in the sun, while

Craggy and windswept, North Cornwall is home to some of the region's most dramatic scenery, such as here at Port Isaac

waves crashing down on the rocks give it a melancholic beauty at other times. It also leads to some quirks of town planning. Lanes (or *opes*, to give them their local appellation) are maddeningly narrow, necessitating complicated and protracted reversing manoeuvres when two cars want to pass each other. Another quirky phenomenon is the town's lower car park, off limits at high tide unless you want your vehicle washed out to sea. There's little in the way of organised attractions here, but the magnificent vistas, plus the whitewashed and slate-fronted fishermen's cottages, make it a wonderful little spot simply to enjoy the timeless Cornish scenery.
27km (17 miles) northeast along the coast from Newquay.

Tintagel

If you didn't know before that Tintagel's main association is with King Arthur, within a minute of reaching this small coastal village you will. Exhaustive efforts have been made to wring every last business opportunity out of the fabled sword-plucker (think Merlins Gifts, The King Arthur's Arms, Excalibur Restaurant and Tea Room, and so forth).

If this irks you, you'll probably also want to skip **King Arthur's Great Halls**. A retired millionaire's 1930s homage to King Arthur's court, it comes with stained-glass windows depicting the legend, a round table (of course) and, somewhat less in keeping with the period, a laser show (*Fore Street. Tel: (01840) 770526. www.kingarthursgreathalls.com. Open: summer 10am–5pm; winter Wed–Sun 11am–3pm, closed second Sat in Oct. Admission charge*).

Opposite, in both senses, is the **Old Post Office**. Formerly a 14th-century manor house, this National Trust property offers a genuine antidote to Tintagel's vein of kitsch (*Fore Street. Tel: (01840) 770024. Open: mid-Feb–Mar & Oct 11am–4pm; Apr & May 10.30am–5pm; Jun–Sept 10.30am–5.30pm. Admission charge*).

Of course, the whole industry has flourished for a very good reason, that being **Tintagel Castle**. Bleak and dramatic, the castle is reachable on foot (or by a Land Rover service), to the west of the village. Ruins from various epochs, unearthed Latin inscriptions and the attached myths and mysteries make for an atmospheric visit, particularly for history buffs (*Tel: (01840) 770328. www.english-heritage. org.uk. Open: Apr–Sept 10am–6pm; Oct 10am–5pm; Nov–Mar 10am–4pm. Admission charge*). Tintagel has a helpful **Visitor Information Centre** (*Bossiney Road. Tel: (01840) 779084. www.visitboscastleandtintagel.com. Open: Mar–Oct 10am–5pm; Nov–Feb 10.30am–4pm*).

5km (3 miles) west along the coast from Boscastle.

North Cornwall

One man and his dog peruse Cornish goodies in a local shop in Port Isaac

King Arthur

With universal themes of love, heroism, chivalry, magic and treachery, it is clear why the legend of King Arthur has exerted such a hold on the public imagination for so long. A composite of various myths and folktales plus texts by Geoffrey of Monmouth, Thomas Malory and many others, few may agree on the finer points of the story but its images of a sword rising from a lake, Camelot and the round table have widespread recognition and currency.

A key figure throughout Arthur's life, it was Merlin – possessed of magic powers through his incubus father – who brought about the king's birth through supernatural means. The boy's father, King Uther, fearing for his son's safety during the ongoing Saxon invasions, entrusted his care to the wizard, who became a lifelong mentor.

On the death of his father, Arthur became king through the Sword in the Stone episode. With no obvious successor for the king due to the boy's secret upbringing, a test was set to determine who would become the new monarch. A sword, known as Excalibur, was set – seemingly fast – in stone. The only person able to pull

the sword from the stone was the rightful king. Many tried and failed. But when Arthur, looking for a sword for his brother, happened upon the scene, he pulled it out easily and ascended to the throne. In another story, the boy was given the weapon by the Lady in the Lake to replace one broken in battle, although this is generally considered a different sword.

Arthur's great success in battle, aided by his indomitable sword, soon won over his critics. He set up court at the (probably fictional) castle of Camelot, which was endowed with a large round table, a wedding present from King Leodegrance of Cameliard when his daughter Guinevere and Arthur married. The best and the bravest knights sought to serve the king, with the elite chosen to sit at the round table, whose shape was symbolic of their equality. Arthur waged triumphant campaigns against the Saxons and in Europe. Meanwhile, his knights pursued the Holy Grail, with varying results.

But the utopia of Camelot was not to last. Bewitched by the Lady of the Lake, Merlin was imprisoned and unable to assist the king. Arthur's

The evocative ruins at Tintagel recall the mythical epoch of King Arthur, with all its chivalry, heroism and betrayal

truest knight and dear friend Sir Lancelot began an affair with Guinevere. After Mordred, the king's villainous nephew, informed his uncle of their trysts, the lovers escaped to Brittany, pursued by the king and his army. Ambitious and impatient, Mordred was already due to succeed to the throne in turn, but he exploited the monarch's absence by claiming that Arthur had been killed. When Arthur learned what his treacherous nephew was doing he returned to England, and the two faced off in the Battle of Camlann. The wronged king slew Mordred but, without the magical protection of Excalibur and its sheath (both stolen by Arthur's half-sister Morgan le Fay), was mortally injured himself.

Knowing he was near death, Arthur commanded one of his knights, Sir Bedivere, to throw the legendary sword back into the lake. As he did so, the Lady of the Lake's hand rose to receive it. Arthur was borne by three queens to the Isle of Avalon, where he died.

South Cornwall

Unlike the north of the county, which is battered by the Atlantic, South Cornwall has a more serene sea. The rivers meeting the English Channel have given rise to several pleasant estuary towns, with a surfeit of azure visible from many well-appointed hotel rooms. Nature is much more orderly on the south coast, offering a selection of neat gardens, pretty meadows and winding country lanes, sheltered by huge hedges.

Though Land's End and St Ives host droves of visitors, other spots in the vicinity are at a slight remove from the main tourist trail, lending them a tranquillity you would struggle to find in, say, Padstow. This is no reflection of their intrinsic value: the history and landscapes of this cliffy corner of the southwest more than repay the effort required to get there.

If it's coastline you seek, the two peninsulas, Lizard and Penwith, have it in bucketfuls – although buckets and spades are generally absent from their far-flung beaches. These two English extremities (respectively, the country's southernmost and westernmost mainland points) have spectacular panoramas, best experienced on the car-free coastal trails beloved of cyclists and hikers. Of the two, Penwith is the busier, hosting as it does Land's End, the starting (or finishing) point of the UK's famous end-to-end journey LEJOG between the acknowledged northernmost point of Scotland, John

o'Groats, and its most distant mainland correspondent.

If Land's End is the southwest's most renowned tourist attraction, South Cornwall also boasts the second: the enormous conservation project built in a former china clay pit, namely the Eden Project. Much of what makes Devon and Cornwall stand out – nature, and a good nose for sustainable tourism – is showcased at this phenomenal site. The two epicentres of the county's artistic life, St Ives and Falmouth, provide further local interest, and the area is also home to Cornwall's amiable capital, Truro.

FALMOUTH

The third-deepest harbour in the world, and the deepest in Western Europe, Falmouth, past and present, is entwined with maritime pursuits. A key port for half a millennium, the area was a potential target for the Spanish Armada, and it was here that Britain first received news of its victory in the

Battle of Trafalgar and the death of Admiral Nelson, with the report relayed to London by stagecoach. Latter-day Falmouth has also been involved in some significant voyages, with record-breaking world-circumnavigators Sir Francis Chichester and Dame Ellen MacArthur both traversing the port.

The zenith of Falmouth's importance on the national stage was during the era of the Falmouth Packet Service from the end of the 17th to the mid-19th centuries, when the town transported mail all over the British Empire. In time, tourism replaced the post, and the port developed as a standard British coastal resort. But recent years have seen another direction for the town, as the Falmouth College of Arts (since re-badged as University College Falmouth) brought creative types flocking to the area, many of whom stayed on after their course and helped create a local artistic community, quite at odds with the ostensibly bland suburban feel of some of the town centre. The student vibe has manifested itself in an abundance of cultural events in film, theatre, music, comedy and academic disciplines such as science, with venues like The Poly (though its future is currently uncertain, see p83) having become thriving arts centres. *13km (8 miles) south of Truro.*

Church of King Charles the Martyr

A simple and pleasant church that was consecrated in 1665, dedicated to the

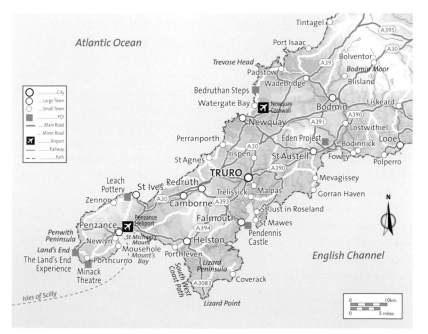

The River Fal, once a target of the invading French and Spanish, today is the site of pleasant boat trips

memory of the executed Charles I, whose oil painting hangs on the south wall. The bright white ceiling differentiates it from some of the gloomier cathedrals in the region. Features of note include the Tuscan columns, stained-glass windows fashioned from 18th-century Italian glass, and an ornate 18th-century font. Dan Brown devotees may be interested to learn that the credence table is rumoured to contain a secret door, which has never been located.
A coffee shop downstairs serves drinks and snacks.
Church Street. Tel: (01326) 313051. Email: kcmvestry@onetel.net.uk. Open: summer Mon–Fri 10am–3pm; year round Thur–Sun services. Free admission.

The Moor

Not a moor in the Bodmin sense of the word, this central square is the heart of Old Falmouth, and has some decent places to eat. It's also from here that the energetic visitor can ascend Jacob's

Ladder, a vertiginous 111-step staircase, whose eponymous builder, Jacob Hamblen, was also a tallow chandler and property owner, and who wanted to be able to move with (relative) ease between his premises. The square's municipal buildings also house the **Falmouth Art Gallery**. Included in the permanent collection are works by Victorian British Impressionists, maritime artists and old masters, while the seasonal exhibitions also showcase contemporary art.
Tel: (01326) 313863. Email: info@ falmouthartgallery.com. www. falmouthartgallery.com. Open: Mon–Sat 10am–5pm. Closed: Sun. Free admission.

National Maritime Museum Cornwall

Maritime matters of every conceivable kind are explored in this large, modern venue which houses the local branch of the Greenwich-based museum. The various rooms and exhibits centre on the Flotilla Gallery, where a collection of vessels is suspended, rather surreally, from the ceiling, with walkways allowing you to inspect them at closer quarters and learn more from the wall panels. Other rooms cover themes from Falmouth's time at the centre of the Packet Service, boat building and repair, and fishing. The museum's location affords superb sea views. *Discovery Quay. Tel: (01326) 313388. www.nmmc.co.uk. Open: 10am–5pm. Admission charge.*

Pendennis Castle

Built at the behest of Henry VIII to defend the mouth of the River Fal from potential incursions by France and Spain, the castle was of strategic importance again during the Civil War, as the scene of a five-month siege. It was in use once more, four centuries after construction, during World War II. The experience of battle is conveyed through interactive exhibits, and you can also explore the secret tunnels. Re-enactments, jousting, concerts and plays are sometimes hosted at the site. *To the east of town. Tel: (01326) 316594. www.english-heritage.org.uk. Open: Apr–Jun & Sept Sun–Fri 10am–5pm, Sat 10am–4pm; Jul–Aug Sun–Fri 10am–6pm, Sat 10am–4pm; Oct–Mar 10am–4pm, certain buildings by guided tour only. Admission charge.*

The Poly

Formerly known as Falmouth Arts Centre, The Poly has three galleries for exhibiting artists, as well as a theatre/cinema. This wonderful venue has traditionally hosted a plethora of events, from music, drama, film and comedy to monthly scientific talks, although since its commercial arm went into liquidation in 2010 its programme has been curtailed, and a fund-raising campaign is under way to try to keep the much loved venue operating. *24 Church Street. Tel: (01326) 212300. www.thepoly.org. Open: usually Mon–Sat 10am–5pm. Closed: Sun. Admission to galleries free.*

Pendennis Castle, built at the command of Henry VIII, now plays host to re-enactments, jousting, concerts and plays

The Eden Project

Approach the Eden Project, the environmental project a few kilometres from St Austell, and what greets you is like a surreal vision of the future. Two tripartite biomes that look akin to enormous golf balls, set in a reclaimed china clay pit, ostensibly have little connection or harmony with the county in which they're located. But this well-run and fascinating place has in a decade become Cornwall's premier tourist attraction.

Former composer Tim Smit had already transformed a derelict space into the **Lost Gardens of Heligan** (*www.heligan.com*) when, in 1994, he hit upon the idea of a site that would showcase humankind's relationship with and dependence on the plant world. The ugly remains of a china clay pit, embodying the destruction being wreaked upon the earth, seemed an appropriate place to transform. In 2001, after an initial investment of £80 million, the site opened its doors to the public.

The giant golf balls are in fact made up of large geodesic hexagons. One section, the Humid Tropics (or Rainforest) Biome, is said to be the largest greenhouse in the world – tall enough to hold the Tower of London or, to use the standard British measurement comparison system, 11 double-decker buses. The tropical plants inside hail from Malaysia, West Africa and South America, and include banana trees, coffee, rubber and bamboo. A big Malaysian trading ship makes the connection with man. The smaller Warm Temperate Biome, mimicking the conditions in the Mediterranean, South Africa and California, is home to olives, grapes and the like, as well as various sculptures. The third 'biome' – basically outside – showcases the tea, lavender, hops and hemp from temperate regions. In total, the site is home to more than a million plants representing 5,000 species from around the world.

But the Eden Project is not merely a glorified botanical garden. At each juncture the attempt is made to outline the links that plants have with humans, and how our survival is contingent on the botanical world. Despite this stated aim, the tone never gets preachy or dogmatic. It's certainly 'right on' – but in the right ways. Food is sourced locally, and there are excellent disabled facilities. If you come by bike or walk you get a discount.

The huge biomes of the Eden Project compose one of Cornwall's top attractions, enthralling young and old alike

Although some displays are designed with children in mind, there is plenty to interest adults too. The main exhibits of the biomes are supplemented by a wealth of other ways to pass the time. Talks, workshops, trails, debates and films are organised. Away from the more serious side, the project stages various entertainment events, the most famous of which is the Eden Sessions, a series of gigs by big names such as Al Murray and Amy Winehouse.

With so much to see – and plenty in the way of facilities, such as a choice of restaurants and (obligatory) pasty outlet – it's already easy to spend a whole day here. But the Eden Project is not – and never will be – the finished article. The Edge, the next planned extension, will focus on sustainability and energy. And energy is what you need to explore this unique attraction.

Bodelva. Tel: (01726) 811911. www.edenproject.com. Open: summer 10am–6pm; winter 10am–4.30pm. Closing times can vary, last admission 90 minutes before closing. Admission charge. 6.5km (4 miles) northeast of St Austell or 28km (17½ miles) east of Truro.

Boat trip: Cruising from Falmouth

With the sea such an integral part of Cornwall, it would be a shame to spend your entire trip on land. A dedicated boat trip will allow you to view the mainland from the sea and imagine yourself in the position of the many mariners, real and imagined – fishermen, smugglers or mermaids.

The distance covered here is 19km (12 miles), about an hour on the boat, or up to a whole day hopping on and off.

Several companies offer trips out of Falmouth: look for advertisements around the town or else head for the Prince of Wales Pier, which is the point of departure. The routes usually encompass most, if not all, of the following destinations. In many cases, your ticket allows you to hop on and hop off, so you can explore each place at leisure.

1 Falmouth

The starting and finishing point for many boat trips over the centuries, including Dame Ellen MacArthur's record-breaking world circumnavigation in 2005. If your thirst for all things maritime is not quenched by your voyage, disembark into the National Maritime Museum, an 800m (875yd) walk down the road (*see pp82–3*).

From Falmouth, the boat will head north. If you're ending your voyage here, the city has a lively arts and entertainment scene so you should be able to find some live music or a good

eatery. However, an alternative boarding/disembarkation point is St Mawes.

The Coinage Hall is one of Truro's historic buildings

2 St Mawes

The other side of the river mouth, St Mawes is primarily known for its castle (*see p109*).

The boat will take you north along the River Fal, for slightly over 8km (5 miles).

3 Trelissick Garden

This peaceful, tiered garden boasts various Mediterranean botanical species and is home to the UK's national collection of photinias and azaras. It also affords great sea and river views, and there is plenty of park and woodland in which to wander. Local arts and crafts are also on show in the gallery.

Feock. Tel: (01872) 862090. www.nationaltrust.org.uk. Open: Feb–Oct 10.30am–dusk or 5.30pm; Nov–Jan 11am–dusk or 4pm. Last admission 30 minutes before closing. Admission charge.

A little way up the river is Tolverne.

4 Tolverne Smugglers Cottage

Prosaically, this thatched cottage was probably originally built for a ferryman rather than a smuggler. Requisitioned by the government during World War II, it served as area headquarters for the Normandy Invasion, and even received the illustrious General Eisenhower. It now operates as a tearoom in the summer months. Some wartime memorabilia is still on view.

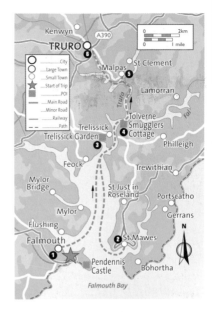

Philleigh. Tel: (01872) 580309. The boat will continue northward. If the tide does not facilitate access to Truro, it will dock at Malpas, and you can continue by bus.

5 Malpas

Scenic Malpas (pronounced Mopus) features in Arthurian legend as the point where Iseult travelled to the palace of her husband King Mark. Its name is said to derive from the French for 'bad crossing'.

Continue, by bus or boat, to Truro.

6 Truro

Cornwall's only city has plenty of cultural and entertainment options (*see pp103–5*).

Finish off your voyage with a meal in town.

Boat trip: Cruising from Falmouth

Mainland England's westernmost point, Land's End is ruggedly beautiful

PENWITH PENINSULA

Dramatic granite cliffs, rugged moors and bright beaches characterise the Penwith Peninsula, appearing on the map like the big toe to Cornwall's foot. The county and country's most western stretch of land is home to the county's most famous geographical feature as well as its artistic nucleus.

Land's End

The name of mainland England's westernmost point is quite self-explanatory. This tip of the country is a windswept wonder, with dramatic cliffs and spectacular sea views. The nature of the beast means that it's always likely to be fairly crowded – unless you time your visit to coincide with the worst weather – but even the touristy atmosphere cannot detract from the magnificence of this promontory. The splendid panorama includes the Irish Lady, Armed Knight and Dr Johnson's Head plus other assorted rocks and reefs arising grandly from the sea, and Longships lighthouse. On a clear day the Isles of Scilly are also visible. Avian life is usually out in force, and extremely fortunate visitors might even spot a dolphin. The famous signpost, pinpointing New York 5,065km (3,147 miles), John O'Groats 1,407km (874 miles), Isles of Scilly 45km (28 miles) and Longships lighthouse 2.5km (1½ miles), with space for your own town or message to be formed from letters in the spare bit, is the classic photo opportunity. Be warned: you may have to queue for it. *Bus: 1, 1A, 345, 300 (summer only). 14.5km (9 miles) west of Penzance.*

The Land's End Experience

While the surroundings here are unequivocally impressive, opinion is split on this small theme park by the site car park. Decried by many as tawdry and inappropriate, on windy days (of which, at Land's End, there are many) you'll probably welcome having some indoor options after exploring the headland. What there is, is certainly fun, and allows you to make a longer trip out of your Land's End sojourn. The main attractions include Doctor Who Up Close (*Open: 10am–4pm*), a joy for fans of the series, and, with its moving Dalek, other assorted Who nemeses and creepy costumes, kitschy fun for anyone else. Coast, a new arrival, is an interactive exhibit about, as the name suggests, the UK's shoreline. Lifeboat simulator Air Sea Rescue (*Open: 10.30am–3.30pm*) champions the local coastguard and Royal National Lifeboat Institution,

while the End to End Story is a more serious display about the many people to have done the LEJOG journey, including fund-raiser Jane Tomlinson and 'naked rambler' Steve Gough. The latest addition is a thrill-packed 4D pirate film, *The Curse of Skull Rock*. Purists may prefer to stick to the scenery, but the Land's End Experience can be diverting enough. *Tel: 0871 720 0044. www.landsend-landmark.co.uk. Open: Easter–Oct 10am–4 or 5pm, later in Aug; Nov–Mar 10.30am–3.30pm. Admission charge includes car parking which otherwise must be paid separately.*

Penzance

The main town on the Penwith Peninsula, temperate Penzance enjoys the shelter of Mount's Bay. However, its exposed position close to the very tip of England put it right in the path of invading foreigners, and repeated sackings at the hands of the Spanish expunged most of the town's medieval features, leaving the prevailing styles Victorian and Regency. Granted a Royal Market by Henry IV, Penzance still retains a certain dignified elegance, while managing not to pander to tourism in the same way as some other Cornish towns.

It developed as a resort thanks to the railway, which arrived in the 1860s, electing Penzance to be the last stop. While the place itself hosts few distinct attractions, its location as the only town of note on its peninsula and the range of accommodation makes it a good base for day trips to Land's End or jaunts to the Isles of Scilly.

40km (25 miles) southwest of Truro.

The Exchange

Six years in the making, Penzance's major new contemporary art space takes its name from its setting, on the ground floor of the old Telephone Exchange. It's a super location, featuring exhibitions of modern art using diverse media.

Princes Street. Tel: (01736) 363715. Email: mail@theexchangegallery.co.uk. www.newlynartgallery.co.uk. Open: summer Mon–Sat 10am–5pm, bank holidays 11am–4pm, closed: Sun; winter Tue–Sat 10am–5pm, closed: Sun & Mon.

Penlee House Gallery and Museum

This Victorian villa is home to a rotating collection of works from many of the artists who made up the local collectives, the Newlyn and Lamorna schools, and a local history display. The gardens, too, are worth a look.

Morrab Road. Tel: (01736) 363625. Email: info@penleehouse.org.uk. www.penleehouse.org.uk. Open: summer Mon–Sat 10am–5pm; winter Mon–Sat 10.30am–4.30pm. Last admission 30 minutes before closing. Closed: Sun. Admission charge.

The exposed location that once saw Penzance devastated by the Spanish today ensures wonderful azure sea views

Despite repeated sackings by the Spanish, Penzance retains many elegant period buildings, such as the Customs House

A FISHY BUSINESS

In his 1968 book *Cornwall, its Mines and Miners*, John R Leifchild wrote: 'Pilchards are to Cornwall what herrings are to Yarmouth, cotton to Manchester, pigs to Ireland, and coals to Newcastle. In fact, it is doubtful if the Cornish people would not perish by inches if pilchards became extinct. If any one wants to know what pilchards are to a town, let him visit St Ives. Seldom have I enjoyed a sea view more, than when descending the hill that overlooks the town of St Ives, which town looks beautiful from the said hill, situated as it is on a finely curved bay, whose sands are very white. But he who wishes to think well of St Ives should depart without entering it; when fairly (or partly) in it, you find it to be a small, old, narrow unpaved (or only paved with flats) hole of a town. From one side to the other of it, in every corner, cottage, lane, loft, room, inn, chapel, and church thereof, there is but one odour, and that is the reeking odour of pilchards!'

St Ives

Sparkling St Ives, whose elevation gives the town wonderful views over the inspiring bay of the same name, is the epicentre of Cornwall's art scene. But it was initially built on something far less glamorous: pilchards, a resource so abundant that one net brought in half a million fish on one day in the 1860s. In time, stocks were depleted, and when the railway line came to the area, so too did Victorian pleasure seekers, and the town began to take off as a tourist resort. Its third main wave of development came through art. Appealing landscapes, plentiful light, peace and quiet and the low cost of living brought artists flocking into the county, and they congregated

Some of the sculptures in the garden of the Barbara Hepworth Museum

in the town, later becoming known as the St Ives School (*see p14*).

Today, their legacy can still be felt, not only in the established galleries but also in the tiny art shops found along the town's narrow alleyways. Some of the street names add further touches of colour: take a walk along Salubrious Terrace, Bethesda Hill, Teetotal Street and The Digey, or meander down Fish Street, another legacy of the town's past.

11.5km (7 miles) north of Penzance.

Barbara Hepworth Museum

One of the key figures in 20th-century British sculpture, Barbara Hepworth was instrumental in the development of modernism in her field. The museum is housed in what was her studio and home, which is little changed since she lived there, up until her death in a fire in 1975. As well as examples of the art itself, letters, reviews, catalogues and photos help explain the background to it. Some of the sculptures are on display in the adjoining garden.

Barnoon Hill. Tel: (01736) 796226. www.tate.org.uk. Open: Mar–Oct 10am–5.20pm; Nov–Feb Tue–Sun 10am–4.20pm. Last admission 20 minutes before closing. Garden closes at dusk, or 4.20pm, whichever is earlier. Admission charge includes entry into Tate St Ives.

Beaches

Large **Porthmeor Beach**, which stretches across the north end of the town, is the main expanse of sand. High water quality and respectable-sized waves bring in the surf crowd. **Porthminster**, to the south, is another popular spot, and can get crowded in the summer. The former has Blue Flag status, denoting its cleanliness, as did the latter until losing its designation in 2010 owing to heavy rainfall. On the other side of 'The Island', not in fact an island at all but a hilly peninsula with a chapel on top, is the tinier **Porthgwidden Beach**, ideal for picnics and paddling.

Leach Pottery

British studio potter Bernard Leach honed his craft in Japan and set up his

Cornish workshop with a Japanese colleague in 1920. He transmitted his view of pottery as a mixture of art, philosophy, design and craft to various pupils from the UK, USA and Canada, who studied at the site. A museum now pays homage to Leach's contribution to 20th-century art, and there are also exhibitions by modern practitioners. In 2008, the studio reopened after a £1.7 million overhaul.

Higher Stennack, 1.2km (¾ mile) outside St Ives on Zennor Road. Tel: (01736) 799703. www.leachpottery.com. Open: Mar–Oct Mon–Sat 10am–5pm, Sun 11am–4pm; Nov–Feb Mon–Sat 10am–4.30pm, Sun 11am–4pm. Last admission 30 minutes before closing. Admission charge.

St Ives Museum

Eclectic and jam-packed collection of local history exhibits put together by devoted amateurs, featuring everything from a stuffed turtle to shipwreck salvage and a replica traditional Cornish kitchen. The building's own history is similarly haphazard, having served variously as a pilchard-packing plant, laundry and cinema, among other things.

Wheal Dream. Tel: (01736) 796005. Open: Easter–Oct Mon–Fri 10am–5pm, Sat 10am–4pm. Admission charge.

St Ives Society of Artists Gallery

Previously the Mariners' Church, the gallery was founded by some of the biggest names from the St Ives

A glance at the picturesque coastline of St Ives explains the allure the town has held for generations of artists

art scene, including Barbara Hepworth and Ben Nicholson. Following the schism in the local collective, it devoted itself mainly to figurative art. There's a high turnover of pieces, while the Mariners Gallery in the crypt hosts private exhibitions.

Norway Square. Tel: (01736) 795582. www.stisa.co.uk. Open: Mar–early Jan Mon–Sat 10.30am–5.30pm, also Sun during high summer 2.30–5.30pm. Free admission.

Tate St Ives

While obviously not on the scale of its London sister galleries, Tate St Ives is an ennobling addition to the local modern art scene, as well as recognition of its importance. The bright white gallery occupies a superb position overlooking the beach. It hosts a full programme of talks, courses and events, and like its

A CORNISH CONUNDRUM

An 18th-century nursery rhyme has made the name of St Ives famous far beyond county borders:

As I was going to St Ives,
I met a man with seven wives,
And every wife had seven sacks,
And every sack had seven cats,
And every cat had seven kits,
Kits, cats, sacks, wives,
How many were going to St Ives?

The poser often gets the listener multiplying by seven, but it is a trick question: only the narrator was going to St Ives, with the large party of wives, cats and so forth presumably coming in the opposite direction. Therefore, the answer is one. The riddle is used by a psychopath to test Bruce Willis in the film *Die Hard with a Vengeance.*

counterparts the top floor is home to an art café. The focus is more local than the two Tates in the capital, with many of the works reflecting scenes from St Ives. But you'll also

The Tate Gallery focuses on local art

Rising majestically from the water just a few hundred metres off the coast, St Michael's Mount has been in use since antiquity

find works from other major artists, some in retrospectives, such as Grayson Perry and Rose Hilton. *Porthmeor Beach. Tel: (01736) 796226. Email: visiting.stives@tate.org.uk. www.tate.org.uk. Open: Mar–Oct 10am–5.20pm; Nov–Feb Tue–Sun 10am– 4.20pm. Last admission 20 minutes before closing. Admission charge includes entry into Barbara Hepworth Museum.*

Trewyn Garden

This centrally located garden manages to avoid the worst of the tourist stampede. Subtropical plants surround a well-manicured lawn, and there are several benches from which to admire the Barbara Hepworth sculpture. *Bedford Road. Tel: (01736) 336605. Open: summer 7.30am–8.30pm; winter 8am–sunset. Free admission.*

St Michael's Mount

Situated 400m (440yd) offshore, the isle of St Michael's Mount can be reached by a cobbled causeway or small ferry, depending on the tide. One of the county's most distinctive landmarks, the Mount, as it's known to locals, has been in use since antiquity. It is thought to be mentioned in several classical texts, which, if true, would make it one of the earliest identified places in Britain and throughout Western Europe. Following periods of religious and military use, it's now a tourist destination for its castle, which stands sentinel at the top of a long climb. Rooms display period fixtures, art and arms from the Middle Ages to the Georgian era. There's nothing about *National Lampoon*, though, despite the presence of a Chevy Chase room! *Mount's Bay. Tel: (01736) 710507. Email: mail@stmichaelsmount.co.uk. www.stmichaelsmount.co.uk. House open: Apr–Oct Sun–Fri 10.30am–5pm; last admission 45 minutes before closing. Garden open: May & Jun Mon–Fri 10.30am–5pm; Jul–Oct Thur & Fri 10.30am–5pm. Admission charge. 6.5km (4 miles) east of Penzance.*

Drive: Southwestern tip of Cornwall

The two peninsulas that compose the southwest point of Cornwall, and mainland England's southernmost and westernmost tips, are home to some of the county's most bewitching landscapes. Abundant in glorious, rugged coastline and untamed moors, the area also includes several interesting towns and cultural hotspots. The total distance is about 140km (85 miles) and this tour will take a whole day.

Start out at Truro. Take the A390 southwest out of Truro and join the A39, which will bring you directly to Falmouth after almost 18km (11 miles).

1 Falmouth

The port is famous for its harbour and maritime activities, as well as its lively arts scene (*see pp80–83*).
Exit the town the same way that you entered, on the A39. After almost 6.5km (4 miles) join the A394, signposted Helston. After around 15km (9 miles) you'll reach Helston. Join the A3083 and follow signs to Lizard. You'll pass small villages and plenty of superb panoramas, should you wish to stop or make a small detour.

2 Lizard Point

Far less touristy than its western equivalent Land's End, Lizard Point is a great spot to enjoy the rugged headland atmosphere without the rigmarole of a theme park and hundreds of other people (*see pp102–3*).

Retrace your route to Helston. Rejoin the A394, travelling in the same direction in which you were initially going. The road merges with the A30, which leads to Penzance.

3 Penzance

The fictional pirates with whom Gilbert and Sullivan connected this town have long gone, but there is still plenty to enjoy in Penzance, including smart Regency and Georgian architecture and some good galleries (*see pp89–90*).
Leave Penzance to the southwest and rejoin the A30, from where Land's End is well signposted.

4 Land's End

One of Britain's most famous places, Land's End is scenic, inspiring and a must-see. Even the high-season crowds will not detract from the awesome spectacle that is England's westernmost headland (*see pp88–9*).
Go back the way you came, but turn right

instead of left at the first fork. If you reach Sennen, you've missed it. Continue on the B3315, and follow signs to Minack.

5 Minack Theatre

A wonderfully atmospheric venue for drama, this cliff-side theatre can also be visited during the day.

Porthcurno. Tel: (01736) 810181. www.minack.com. Open: Apr–mid-Sept 9.30am–5.30pm (or noon before afternoon show); mid-Sept–Oct 9.30am–5pm; Nov–Mar 10am–4pm. Last admission 30 minutes before closing. Admission charge.

Go back towards Land's End but turn right onto the A30 before you get there. After 3km (2 miles) turn left onto the B3306 and follow signs for St Just.

6 St Just

The ancient mining town of St Just is now another artistic Cornish outpost. As well as the interesting Lafrowda festival, its granite cottages (a legacy of the mining era) and splendid views make it worth a stop.

Return to Penzance on the A3071, then rejoin the A30. After about 21km (13 miles) in total, turn off onto the A3074 and follow signs to St Ives.

7 St Ives

This artistic hub has galleries galore, fine restaurants and a range of accommodation options (*see pp91–5*). *St Ives is a good place to overnight. Alternatively, you can return to Truro.*

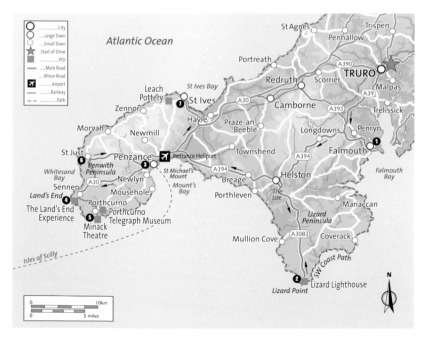

The rugged peninsula abounds with dramatic ocean views

The rest of the peninsula

Penwith certainly has a steady tourist flow, with visitors heading for Land's End, but the area also affords plenty of opportunity to get off the beaten track. Remote villages with no mobile phone reception, tiny winding lanes and villages that, except for the presence of the cars, look much as they would have 50 or 100 years ago, make excellent spots to unwind. Among the highlights are **Newlyn**, Cornwall's biggest fishing port and home to its first colony of artists. This aspect of the town's cultural life is celebrated at **Newlyn Art Gallery**, whose Victorian building belies its modern interior (*24 New Road. Tel: (01736) 363715. www.newlynartgallery.co.uk. Open: summer Mon–Sat 10am–5pm; winter Tue–Sat 10am–5pm. Free admission).* Cobbled streets and the artists in residence hark back to the town's cultural heyday, and you'll also see reminders in the nomenclature, such as the street name Rue des Beaux Arts.

Close to Newlyn and Penzance lies **Mousehole** (another of those deceptive pronunciations – it's articulated as 'Mow-zle'). Once a thriving fishing port, it's now a hub of second homes, with estimates that around half of the residences here are holiday getaways. A brief look will account for its popularity: Mousehole is held by many to be among the most beautiful villages in the county. Come over Christmas and you'll see the town's famous illuminations.

The tiny **Zennor**, the last parish in Britain alphabetically, is another super getaway. Wonderful views of rolling fields before scintillating sea led writer D H Lawrence to describe it as 'a tiny granite village nestling under high

DEATH OF A LANGUAGE

Like Britain's other Celtic and minority languages, Cornish has been ravaged by the inexorable march of English. Following a recent revival project, it is estimated that around 2,000 people now speak the Cornish tongue. The last monoglot (speaker of one language alone) is believed to have been Dolly Pentreath, a resident of Penwith, the bastion of Cornish as a community language. Many tales of Dolly cast her as a crone, swearing at people in anger. When she died in 1777, her last words are said to have been: '*Me ne vidn cewsel Sawznek!*' They translate as: 'I don't want to speak English!'

remote village can be picked up and studied in more detail.
Tel: (01736) 796945. Open: Apr–Oct 10.30am–5.30pm. Closed: Nov–Mar. Admission charge.

The **Porthcurno Telegraph Museum**, just under 5km (3 miles) from Land's End, is also worth a quick visit. The former World War II communications bunker depicts the history of telecoms in the area, and there are regular demonstrations in the tunnels.
Eastern House, Porthcurno. Tel: (01736) 810966. www.porthcurno.ex.ac.uk. Open: Easter–early Nov 10am–5pm (Easter–mid-Sept Wed 10am–7.30pm); mid-Nov–Easter Sun & Mon 10am–5pm. Last admission one hour before closing. Admission charge.

shaggy moor hills, and a big sweep of lovely sea, lovelier even than the Mediterranean… It is the best place I have been in, I think.' It is home to the **Wayside Folk Museum**, some of whose many exhibits on the traditions of the

Homely cottages miles off the beaten track make Mousehole ideal for a getaway

Smuggling

Along with saints, Arthurian knights and assorted artists and writers, the figure perhaps most associated with Cornwall is the smuggler. Miles of exposed coast dotted with secluded inlets and hidden coves, with few officers patrolling them, made the county a fertile transit route for contraband. A sideline for centuries, smuggling became an economic mainstay for many towns, sometimes even eclipsing fishing. 'The coasts here swarm with smugglers from the Land's End to the Lizard,' commented one writer in 1753.

Although smuggling had been documented as early as the 12th century, it came into its own towards

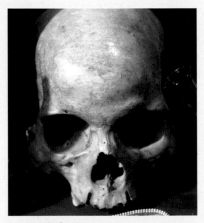
A grisly relic from Jamaica Inn

the end of the 1700s. Britain was waging costly wars against France and America, and needed to fill its war chest. The government's solution was to raise duties on alcohol and other luxury goods being imported from the continent, thus creating a potentially lucrative black market for otherwise struggling mariners. Contraband included tea, brandy, gin, rum and tobacco, with black market prices sometimes as low as one-fifth or one-sixth of the legal cost. It was estimated that half of the brandy and a quarter of all the tea smuggled into the UK came through Devon and Cornwall. China, silk and cotton were also illegally imported. Anything that had high taxes imposed was fair game – Pepper Cove near Porthcothan got its name from the many spices that were landed there.

In the early days, smuggling was a relatively open affair, with consignments simply unloaded onto the shore. This lack of clandestinity was made possible by the involvement of the entire townsfolk. Complicity – and cuts – often reached high society: the Killigrew family, who developed Falmouth, are said to have made their fortune through smuggling and piracy. But from 1800, revenue officials stepped up their efforts against the trade, sending smuggling underground, often literally, with tunnels excavated and coves employed for the purpose.

Dozens of coastal towns were involved. In Mousehole, widespread bribery (and when that failed, pelting with stones) of officials allowed the perpetrators to work with impunity. One customs man described local bootlegger Richard 'Doga' Pentreath as 'an honest man in all his dealings though a notorious smuggler'. Off Mount's Bay a government vessel was fired on when it tried to intercept some illegal cargo. Falmouth's Packet Service was instrumental in the trade, and a fortnight-long market was held on an incoming boat in 1762, where customers could pick up cut-price Chinese silk, china, tea and the like. The most famous smuggling transit point, thanks to Daphne du Maurier's novel of the same name, is probably Jamaica Inn, its remote location ideal for furtive comings and goings.

Across Cornwall, different methods and attitudes earned smugglers differing reputations. John Carter, who became known as the King of Prussia, once broke into a customs house to retrieve a cargo of his that had been seized. 'John Carter has been here,' one of the customs

Exhibits from Jamaica Inn

officers is said to have concluded. 'We know it because he has taken nothing away that was not his own.' Another gang, led by Melchisideck Kinsman, was accused of murdering an excise officer at Porthleven. And while some, like the unfortunate Robert Long, were executed for their crimes, others were acquitted (often with help from bribed or 'nobbled' juries) and lived out their lives free from the sword of justice.

Increasing law enforcement and the reduction of excises to more reasonable levels had taken the bottom out of the market by the mid-19th century, and though there is still the occasional drugs haul, Cornish smuggling lives on now largely in mythology and myriad tourist attractions.

South Cornwall

LIZARD POINT AND PENINSULA

Once the downfall of legions of seafarers, Lizard Peninsula is a less traversed alternative to Penwith. It too contains an extremity – mainland Britain's southernmost point – but lacking a John O'Groats-style counterpoint, it receives far less attention and consequently fewer tourists, making The Lizard a mellower place to visit. It's certainly not the landscape that's responsible for the smaller visitor numbers. The peninsula is rich in the kind of timeless vistas that typify Cornwall at its best. The Loe, or Looe Pool, the county's largest natural freshwater lake, on the west coast close to Helston, is said to be the lake into which Sir Bedivere cast Excalibur at King Arthur's behest. The accuracy of the claim is doubtful, but what is beyond debate is the abundance of wildlife dwelling there. The peninsula also boasts surf and swimming beaches, as well as delightfully tiny hamlets with just a clutch of homes.

Your main port of call, though, is sure to be Lizard Point, the southern tip of the peninsula and country. There is some tourist infrastructure, in the form of a handful of small shops and cafés, but nothing on the scale of Land's End. Walk to the southernmost tip and you could be entirely by yourself, with the sea one side of you and the rest of Britain the other. There's also a steepish walk down to a small stony beach, at low tide. The last spot from which ships could get news from land, Lizard Point was of prime importance in

Less famous than its western counterpart, Lizard Point offers stupendous scenery without the tourist hordes

communications, and it was from near here that the approaching Armada is said to have first been detected. Bright white **Lizard Lighthouse**, the main landmark in the area, dates from 1752. Its predecessor lasted from just 1619 to 1623, having fallen into disrepair due to its inability to collect funds from passing ships.

Tel: (01255) 245011. Open: Apr Sun–Thur 11am–5pm; May & Jun Sun–Thur 10.30am–5pm; Jul Sun–Fri 10.30am–6pm; Aug 10.30am–6.30pm; Sept Sun–Fri 10.30am–5pm; Oct Sun–Wed 11am–4pm; Nov, Dec, Feb & Mar Sun–Wed 11am–3pm.

Admission charge.

29km (18 miles) southeast of Penzance.

TRURO

Cornwall's only city, Truro feels pleasantly non-urban, due in the main to its size (a population of just over 20,000) and bucolic touches such as cobbled streets and mews-style cottages. It achieved its status in the county thanks to its position as a port, facilitating the shipping of tin and copper to the home countries and Europe. The silting of the Truro River, and the town's ensuing declining prosperity, proved but a temporary setback. Tin mining brought the good times back to Truro, and their legacy is clear in its graceful Georgian and Victorian town houses. The elite of the time began to congregate in the town, which became known as 'the London of Cornwall'. High society's

Truro's tranquillity and verdure belie its city status

approval was conferred with the bestowal of city status by Queen Victoria in 1877.

In recent times, Truro has seen many of its small boutiques and businesses replaced with chain stores. Though this is typical of many British towns, locals decry the city's loss of identity (which gave rise to idiosyncrasies like the name Squeeze Guts Alley). While being a river port rather than a coastal port was once an advantage for Truro, sheltering it from foreign invasion, it now means that tourists are unlikely to stay for too long in the town, preferring to head for the beach. However, this charming city is worth a quick stop, not least for its striking cathedral, comprehensive museum and vibrant entertainment scene.

66km (41 miles) west of Plymouth.

It may jar architecturally with the rest of the town, but Truro's neo-Gothic cathedral is an awesome sight

Royal Cornwall Museum

This vast collection goes at depth into all manner of themes including archaeology, biology, geology, decorative and applied arts, coins, social history and world cultures. Artwork by members of the Cornish schools is also in evidence. Temporary exhibitions run the gamut from global to local and can touch on anything and anyone from Leonardo da Vinci to *Poldark*'s Cornwall. The Courtney Library, which holds manuscripts, photographs, engravings and ephemera, requests that visitors call ahead.
River Street. Tel: (01872) 272205. Email: enquiries@royalcornwallmuseum.org.uk. www.royalcornwallmuseum.org.uk. Open: Mon–Sat 10am–4.45pm. Last admission 4.30pm. Closed: Sun and bank holidays. Free admission, but there is sometimes a charge for special exhibitions.

Truro Cathedral

This neo-Gothic cathedral may be an architectural aberration in the city, the designer's choice of the Early English style juxtaposed with the rest of Truro's prevailing Georgianism, but that does not diminish its visual impact. Finished as late as 1910, this was the first new cathedral to be constructed in the UK since St Paul's in London. Struggling to fit into the space allotted, the church feels tall, long and thin. It's a peaceful, atmospheric place, whose most striking feature is perhaps its Victorian stained-glass windows. Consult the website to see the cathedral's impressive range of events, which includes organ recitals, concerts, lectures, films and exhibitions.
14 St Mary's Street. Tel: (01872) 276782.

www.trurocathedral.org.uk. Open: Mon–Sat 7.30am–6pm, Sun 9am–7pm, bank holidays from 9.30am. Free admission, but recommended donation.

POLPERRO

The fishing port of Polperro is one of the almost impossibly picturesque Cornish villages that seems to have managed to elude much of what characterises the modern age. The harbour, rambling stream and neat little cottages are exactly the kind that adorn souvenir biscuit tins and their like. The village's car-free status (during the day in summertime it is practically impossible, and unnecessary, to bring a vehicle into the centre), with tram-cum-milk floats and horses and carts the standard transport, adds to its quaintness.

The town's mainstay was traditionally fishing. It was a pilchard fishing and processing port for hundreds of years, but falling stocks in the 20th century prompted a switch to other species, and today around a dozen commercial vessels haul home scallops, crabs, monkfish and cod, among other things. While the industry itself is much diminished, its presence confers an authenticity that adds to Polperro's allure. But the English village charm conceals a seamy history. Although the official trade was fishing, many fishermen dabbled in the profitable sideline of smuggling. Contraband was passing through the port as early as the 12th century, but

the high taxes imposed to fund Britain's war chest for campaigns against America and France in the 18th century saw a spike in the alcohol and tobacco entering the port illicitly.

With its two main trades receding into the past, Polperro turned to tourism. Though its small size means it can get overrun at the height of summer, visit outside high season and you'll not fail to see what the fuss is about. For those keen to get away from the centre, guided walks in the summer start from the Village Hall. Further details can be found at the tourist office in Looe (*tel: (01503) 262072*), a similarly pretty town 6.5km (4 miles) to the east, and also worthy of exploration.

28km (17½ miles) west of Plymouth.

Polperro exudes old-world, bucolic charm

Cornish mythology

Cornwall's antediluvian traditions, its location (at a slight remove from the rest of mainland Britain) and its rural make-up laid the groundwork for a rich vein of myth. More to do with Celtic folklore than the Germanic-influenced body of mythology in the rest of the country, Cornish legends draw on the natural and manmade environment, such as the sea, moors and mines, along with the ancient relics and buildings still standing throughout the county.

Many of the tales have at their heart the juxtaposition of little and big people, thought to have derived from the mixing of the tall Celts with the smaller, local people. Cornish giants are often associated with the large stone circles of the county. Tales are manifold, but the giants are often depicted as bothersome. Bolster, who was able to stand with one foot on Carn Brea, a hill outside Camborne, and the other 10km (6 miles) away on cliffs near St Agnes, was one such nuisance, terrorising local people. After many tried vainly to vanquish him, he found his nemesis in innocent Saint Agnes, with whom he fell in love and then pursued. Exasperated by his attentions, Agnes challenged him to prove his love by filling a pool with his blood. What Bolster didn't know was that the pool led to the sea. He bled to death, with the red marks on the cliffs at Chapel Porth said to pay testimony.

Other malevolent leviathans included Cormoran, the Giant of St Michael's Mount, who was tricked into falling into a pit and killed, and The Wrath of Portreath, who hurled stones at ships and dragged them out of the sea. He would then feed on the fat sailors, throwing the thin ones away.

At the other end of the scale were the little people. Inch-high *piskies* (the Cornish word for pixies), who dressed in waistcoats and stockings, were good-natured, helping the elderly, although not immune to playing a prank or two. Hideous-looking Spriggans, on the other hand, kidnapped babies, summoned storms to spoil the harvest and harassed solo travellers. Mine-dwelling Knockers were benevolent while being fed with pasty scraps, but could bring misfortune to anyone who wronged them.

With the sea so omnipresent, the mermaid, too, is a stock figure in Cornish folklore. Legend has it that a Zennor man, Mathew Trewella,

Boscastle's absorbing Museum of Witchcraft showcases a weird and wonderful selection of memorabilia of the spirit world

sang at church so mellifluously that a mermaid from nearby Pendour Cove was spellbound. She began to attend the church, covering her tail with a long dress, and soon the pair fell in love. But the mermaid had to return to the sea or she would die. Mathew was so in love that he vowed to go with her, and the couple went into the water, never to emerge. It is said that his singing is sometimes audible at Pendour Cove on the breeze.

The legacy lives on. Cornwall has several 'haunted' houses, and its overtones of the menacing and supernatural are drawn on in literature such as Daphne du Maurier's novels and the films of The House of Fear film studio.

Polperro Heritage Museum of Smuggling and Fishing

The town's two lifebloods are explored in this small museum, a former pilchard factory to the east of the harbour. Exhibits date from the 18th century, and include photos, replica boats, pilchard paraphernalia and artwork. The story of the *Lottery*, a notorious smuggling vessel whose crew murdered a customs official, is also depicted, along with a cutlass belonging to one of the gang.

The Warren. www.polperro.org.
Open: Mar–Oct daily 11am–5pm.
Admission charge.

FOWEY

Upmarket and popular with well-heeled second-homers, Fowey can probably be described as the south coast's equivalent of Padstow. You'll mark yourself immediately as an outsider if you articulate the town's name as it reads; the correct pronunciation is 'Foy'. Once the main port on Cornwall's south coast, the town derived its prosperity from its maritime role, first as a military garrison and later for exports. Boats still negotiate their way in and out of the harbour today, although the freighters and trawlers have now been joined by the posh yachts of the smart set. Such luminaries as TV hosts Richard and Judy are among the many high-net-worth buyers to have sent the local property market rocketing. It's certainly clear what motivates them. The town is hilly and pretty, with narrow winding streets, and the influx of moneyed residents has got boutiques and upmarket eateries popping up through the town, in

Fowey's picturesque houses have made it a magnet for well-heeled second-homers

The castle at St Mawes stands sentinel over the English Channel

particular on Fore Street. It's a peaceful place, in which glorious river views are set off by birdsong.

But while Fowey might top the holiday-home list for today's celebrities, its main association is with a far more eminent figure. Writer Daphne du Maurier lived at Menabilly, a remote manor house close to town, which served as the inspiration for Manderley, the ominous mansion of her novel *Rebecca*. An arts and literature festival in honour of the author is held in and around the town every year. There are some excellent coastal walks to be had in the vicinity, too, providing the ideal scenery for imagining you are the second Mrs de Winter or a dashing du Maurier hero.

36km (22 miles) west of Plymouth.

ST MAWES

Visitors pitch up at the isolated town of St Mawes, which lies opposite Falmouth, mainly for the castle. Built in the 16th century, the fortress's lack of action (it quickly capitulated to the parliamentarian forces in the English Civil War) means it stands today in superb condition. Excellent views, ominous oubliettes and the gun installations are the highlights. The free audio guide fills you in on the history. *A3078. Tel: (01326) 270526. www.english-heritage.org.uk. Open: Apr–Jun & Sept Sun–Fri 10am–5pm; Jul & Aug Sun–Fri 10am–6pm; Oct daily 10am–4pm; Nov–Mar Mon & Fri–Sun 10am–4pm. Admission charge. 11.5km (7 miles) south of Truro.*

Daphne du Maurier

The fact that Daphne du Maurier was, by birth, a Londoner, rather than a native Cornwallian, seems to have had little impact on the way her life and works are inextricably bound up in the fabric of the county. From providing the settings of some of her most iconic novels to the location of her home and now an annual arts and literature festival paying homage to her, the writer's life can be mapped out on Cornwall.

Born in 1907, du Maurier first came to Cornwall in the 1920s, when her well-to-do parents bought a holiday home (in the days before such wealthy 'incomers' were resented!) in Bodinnick near Fowey. While at the property, now called Ferryside, the fledgling author penned her first novel, at the age of 22. *The Loving Spirit* was a saga centring on a family of shipbuilders and mariners from the (fictitious) Cornish village of Plyn. Though the title was not one of her biggest successes, it had an unexpected pay-off for du Maurier's personal life. One reader, a military man named Sir Frederick Browning, was so moved by the book that he sailed to Fowey to meet its creator in person. The two were soon married.

The couple did not immediately choose to reside in Cornwall, but visited for holidays. On one occasion, du Maurier became lost when horse riding on a foggy Bodmin Moor, and was forced to spend the night at Jamaica Inn. There, the local rector is said to have told her tales of ghosts and smuggling. The result is the novel named after the hotel, a dark tale of

The inn that inspired du Maurier's dark tale of wreckers is one of several Cornish sights linked to the author

Du Maurier's works have been translated into over 20 languages and spawned various screen adaptations

a gang of wreckers. *Jamaica Inn* spawned a 1939 Alfred Hitchcock adaptation (which du Maurier disliked), stage show and TV version.

In 1943, ten years into their marriage, the writer and her husband decided to move to Cornwall full-time. She would later write of the place: 'Here was the freedom I desired, long sought-for, not yet known… Freedom to write, to walk, to wander, freedom to climb hills, to pull a boat, to be alone.' After briefly renting a property in Fowey, the couple took out a 25-year lease on a 17th-century mansion du Maurier had first seen years earlier. Menabilly, which overlooked the sea, was the inspiration for Manderley, the gothically sinister pile still seemingly haunted by the ghost of the owner's

late wife in *Rebecca*. The novel's first line, 'Last night I dreamt I went to Manderley again', must be one of the most identifiable openers in English literature. Hitchcock was again entrusted with the screen adaptation, which went on to win an Oscar.

When the lease on the immortalised Menabilly expired, du Maurier, now a widow, took another property owned by the same family a couple of kilometres away. Kilmarth earned the same treatment as Manderley as a location in a later novel, *The House on the Strand*, albeit with far less impact on the public consciousness. Made a dame in 1969, the author spent the rest of her life at the house. After her death in 1989, her ashes were scattered on the cliffs nearby.

Getting away from it all

Isolated hamlets, rugged moorland and miles of blue sea... Devon and Cornwall certainly offer plenty of opportunity to escape from the daily grind, get some pristine air in your lungs and behold the full glory of nature. This can be done the easy way – from wherever you are, a short drive is usually enough to reach a rural outpost – or the 'hard' way: hitting the high seas or taking flight to one of the peninsula's islands.

ISLANDS
The Isles of Scilly

Situated 45km (28 miles) southwest of Land's End, the Isles of Scilly take the tranquillity, sunshine and prettiness of Cornwall to even more wonderful extremes. No fixed total has been agreed upon – it depends upon the definition used and the tide – but the archipelago is said to consist of between 100 and 150 islets. None is larger than 5km (3 miles) in diameter, and only five are inhabited (six if you count Gugh, which had a population of three in the most recent census). Many of the remainder are home to wildlife colonies, some of which can be visited.

With no traffic, and well off the standard tourist trail, the peace and quiet here is punctuated only by birdsong. The islands enjoy a balmy microclimate, with the sea protecting them from the worst excesses of frost and snow. There's also plenty of sunshine (the name 'Scilly' is thought to be derived from Roman and Viking words meaning 'sun'). However, exposure to Atlantic winds can result in dramatic winter gales. The effects of the generally warm weather are apparent in the plantlife: the verdant subtropical Abbey Gardens top the list of tourist attractions. Flower farming is the second string in the archipelago's economic bow, after

LITTLE LEAGUE

As well as being home to the most athletic population in the UK, according to a 2006 Sport England survey, the Isles of Scilly also host what is believed to be the smallest football league in the world. Two teams – Woolpack Wanderers and Garrison Gunners – play each other 16 times a season in the league and also contest two cups. The same referee officiated at every game for over 15 years. At the end of the season, players are redistributed to keep the competition even, and the title is frequently decided on the last day of the season. Football and travel writer Charlie Connelly noted: 'Lots of people turn up and sing "Can we play you every week?" and each thinks they are the first to think of it.'
www.worldssmallestleague.co.uk

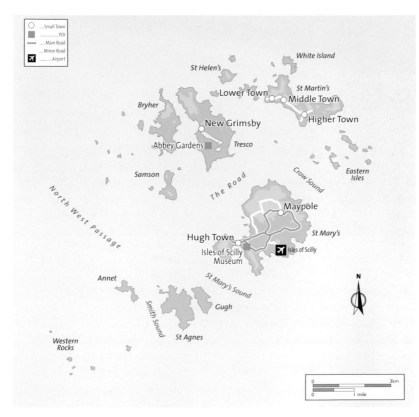

tourism, and in spring the effect is quite beautiful.

The main action is on the largest and most populous island, St Mary's, whose capital is Hugh Town. The 'off islands' – locals' name for the four other inhabited patches of land – are Tresco, St Martin's, St Agnes and Bryher. Passengers can travel between the main group on inter-island launches operated by the **St Mary's Boatmen's Association** (*www.scillyboating.co.uk*). The archipelago is reached in the first place by ferry or plane (*www.islesofscilly-travel.co.uk*), with a reduced schedule in winter and services on only a couple of Sundays throughout the year. You can also get there by helicopter (*www.islesofscillyhelicopter.com*). When booking your ticket, and in general on the island, remember to use the name Isles of Scilly – Scilly Isles and Scillies are considered Scillonian *faux pas*.

Abbey Gardens

This gloriously lush garden is home to 20,000 exotic plants from 80 countries ranging from Brazil to Burma.
Tresco. Tel: (01720) 424105. Open: daily 9.30am–4pm. Admission charge.

'The longer one stays here the more does the spirit of the moor sink into one's soul, its vastness, and also its grim charm,' wrote Sir Arthur Conan Doyle of Dartmoor

Isles of Scilly Museum

The diverse collection includes many items salvaged from ships or simply washed up on the shore.

Church Street, St Mary's. Tel: (01720) 422337. www.iosmuseum.org. Open: Easter–Sept Mon–Fri 10am–4.30pm; Oct–Easter Mon–Sat 10am–noon. Admission charge.

Lundy Island

Though on far less grand a scale than the Isles of Scilly, Lundy offers a similarly timeless appeal. Lying about 19km (12 miles) off the coast of Devon, it's quicker to reach than the archipelago, and in summer can be done as a day trip; indeed, that's what most visitors choose. Exuding rustic appeal, Lundy is home to Devon's only puffin nesting place, plus various other wildlife – sometimes including basking sharks. Landmarks come in the form of

a castle, two lighthouses, some inscribed stones and a pub.

NATIONAL PARKS AND MOORS
Dartmoor National Park

Wild and wonderful Dartmoor, southern England's greatest wilderness, combines the stunning natural beauty of its moorland with ancient sites, activities and a dense layer of mythology. Its geography includes tors (large, granite hills), copious rivers (thanks to the high rainfall) and woods, all of which add to the mood and mystery in which the place is steeped. A plethora of wildlife is headed by the flagship Dartmoor ponies, but abundant other mammals and livestock also call the moors home, as does a long list of avian residents. Relics pay testament to the park's history, with spooky ancient monuments adding to the atmosphere, which Sir Arthur

Conan Doyle's brooding thriller *The Hound of the Baskervilles* perfectly encapsulates.

In his novel Doyle described Dartmoor as 'this most God-forsaken corner of the world. (…) When you are once out upon its bosom you have left all traces of modern England behind you, but, on the other hand, you are conscious everywhere of the homes and the work of the prehistoric people. On all sides of you as you walk are the houses of these forgotten folk, with their graves and the huge monoliths which are supposed to have marked their temples. As you look at their gray stone huts against the scarred hillsides you leave your own age behind you, and if you were to see a skin-clad, hairy man crawl out from the low door

fitting a flint-tipped arrow on to the string of his bow, you would feel that his presence there was more natural than your own.'

As well as camping, to which the environment obviously lends itself, more comfortable accommodation comes in the form of homely old inns. The main fun is to be had outdoors, but there are a few interesting indoor attractions.

Dartmoor Prison Museum
Confiscated contraband, such as a knife fashioned from matchsticks, are among the most interesting items on display, along with a rather gruesome flogging frame and paintings by prisoners. The helpful staff will happily answer questions.

Modern-day Dartmoor seems little changed from its mythical past

Princetown, next to prison. Tel: (01822) 322130. www.dartmoor-prison.co.uk. Open: Mon–Thur & Sat 9.30am–12.30pm & 1.30–4.30pm, Fri & Sun 9.30am–12.30pm & 1.30–4pm. Last admission 30 minutes before closing. Admission charge.

Museum of Dartmoor Life

This three-floor museum takes an extensive look at the people who have inhabited Dartmoor since time immemorial and the ways in which they sustained themselves.
3 West Street, Okehampton.
Tel: (01837) 52295.
www.museumofdartmoorlife.eclipse.co.uk.
Open: Easter–Oct Mon–Sat 10.15am–4.30pm; opening hours vary in winter.
Admission charge.

A charming waterfall in the picturesque Exmoor village of Winsford

Okehampton Castle

Devon's largest castle – or what is left of it – enjoys a fine position above the River Okement. From its origins as a motte and bailey castle following the Norman Conquest, with mention made of it in the Domesday Book, it came into the possession of the Earl of Devon, Hugh Courtenay. When his heir further down the line was beheaded at Henry VIII's behest, for conspiring against the government, the luxury residence began its decline, and is now said to be haunted. Visitors can explore the woods or picnic by the river, while the free audio guides give further details about the castle.
1.5km (1 mile) southwest of Okehampton town centre. Tel: (01837) 52844. www.english-heritage.org.uk. Open: Apr–Jun & Sept 10am–5pm; Jul & Aug 10am–6pm. Closed: Oct–Mar. Admission charge.

A dramatic natural rock formation on Bodmin Moor

Exmoor National Park

Not as wild as Dartmoor, Exmoor straddles Devon and Somerset, lying largely (over two-thirds) in the latter. Its 55km (34 miles) of coastline add to the marvellous views in the park itself. The variety of wildlife is a highlight, from Exmoor ponies (rides on which are always a favourite with children) to red deer, sheep and numerous birds. Exmoor's main literary link is with Richard Doddridge Blackmore's dashing romance *Lorna Doone*.

Bodmin Moor

It may lack national park status, but the granite moorland of Bodmin is marked by dramatic tors, prehistoric stone circles and bogs, giving it a preternatural appeal. Its two main associations – Jamaica Inn, inspiration for the gothic du Maurier novel of the same name, and as the home to the

legendary Beast of Bodmin (*see pp122–3*) – add to the spookiness.

Jamaica Inn

Attached to the hotel, this quaint and wonderfully old-fashioned museum hosts an array of du Maurier memorabilia as well as a fabulous – and sometimes quite macabre – display on smuggling, featuring a smuggler's skull and mummified mouse. The array of contraptions and disguises used to conceal contraband – including camel saddle, turban, life jacket, turtle shell and hollowed-out copy of the *AA Members Handbook* – is a bewildering testament to the smugglers' audacity and ingenuity. *Bolventor. Tel: (01566) 86250. www.jamaicainn.co.uk. Open: Easter–Sept, excluding school holidays 10am–5pm; school holidays 10am–6pm; Oct–Dec & Feb–Easter 11am–4pm. Closed: Jan. Admission charge.*

Walk: Dartmoor

There really is an infinite number of potential walks on Dartmoor. Some are guided, on others it will just be you and the great outdoors. Some are undemanding strolls, others negotiate tough peaks and troughs. The park's official website (www.dartmoor-npa.gov.uk) is a good place to start.

This 10.5km (6¹/₂-mile) walk will take around four hours.

If you're getting to this walk by car, park in Dartmeet, where the walk ends; you can then collect your car at the finishing point. From here, take the bus to Dunnabridge, asking the driver to let you off at Dunnabridge Pound.

1 Dunnabridge Pound
Dunnabridge Pound dates from prehistoric times and was used to keep cattle.
Enter the gate and take the public bridleway towards Laughter Hole Farm. Proceed along the track until you reach the gate that will eventually lead to Bellever. At the fork, bear right.

2 Laughter
Scene of a farmhouse, Laughter Hole Farm, a tor and a standing stone. The stone row close to the last is slightly obscured by undergrowth.
From Laughter Hole Farm, continue along to the bridleway towards Bellever until the path starts to curve to the left as it descends the hill.

Continue the way you were walking until you see a gate on your right, marked 'path'. Enter it, and follow the path past a picnic area and other facilities to your left.

3 Bellever
Just 1.5km (1 mile) southwest of Bellever, Bellever Tor, surrounded by coniferous forests, affords superb views over the south of the park on a clear day. The area also boasts significant remains of former settlements, including tombs and stone rows.
Cross the bridge, go right on the road and continue around the base of Riddon Ridge.

4 Riddon Ridge
Its name a derivative of 'red down', if you go in summer this area will have a glorious russet heather coating. Other highlights include several prehistoric remains, such as hut settlements and cairns.
After some 2km (1¹/₄ miles) the road becomes part of the Two Moors Way. Pass

the left-hand turn for Middle Cator and leave the road via the track to the right at the bend. It joins the road at Sherwell.

5 Sherwell

The hamlet of Sherwell, or Sherrill as it is sometimes called, is home to some pretty old cottages.

At the junction (facing the same direction as before) turn right and continue along the road for 100m (110yd). Mount the ladder stile and then, staying to the left of the field, go

through the gate at the bottom and cross the stream using the footbridge. Follow the path through the trees to another gate and field, through which is Yar Tor.

6 Yar Tor

Made up of three main piles and an extensive clitter field, the name 'yar' probably comes from 'hart', from the time when deer were more abundant. The tor offers good views.

Follow the track back to the car park and bus stop, where you can enjoy a cream tea.

Walk: Dartmoor

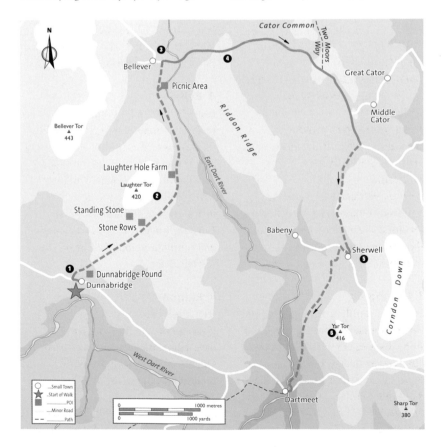

Walk: Exmoor Tarr Steps

Like Dartmoor, Exmoor has no end of walks for all levels of proficiency and energy. This route includes a couple of the moor's prettiest villages, two natural attractions supposedly made by the devil himself, a few ancient constructions and some superb moor panoramas.

The 32km (20-mile) walk is likely to take a day if you factor in a pub lunch and some sit-downs. The Ordnance Survey map OL9 Exmoor would be useful.

Take the B3222 or the bus to Dulverton.

1 Dulverton

Countrified Dulverton dates back to Saxon times. Winding, medieval streets and charming old buildings characterise the town, mention of which was made in the Domesday Book. There's also the **Guildhall Heritage Centre** if you want to linger (*Monmouth Terrace. Open: Apr–Oct 10am–4.30pm. Free admission*). **The Exmoor National Park Centre** is the place to find out more about the national park (*7–9 Fore Street. Tel: (01398) 323841. www.exmoor-nationalpark.gov.uk. Open: Apr–Oct 10am–1.15pm & 1.45–5pm; Nov–Mar 10.30am–3pm. Free admission*). *Starting at the bridge crossing the River Barle in Dulverton, take the riverside path upstream to Tarr Steps.*

2 Tarr Steps

This prehistoric clapper bridge was possibly built as early as 1000 BC

(although some historians believe it to be medieval). It is held by many to be the best of its kind in the country. According to local legend, the devil himself built the bridge as a sunbathing spot. Unfortunately, he failed to take into account the silting of the River Barle, and the bridge is now sometimes underwater, which not only has deleterious effects on the gritstone but sometimes sees the slabs washed away (which must then be retrieved and repaired). The ancient woodland around the site also merits exploration, not least for the potential plethora of wildlife spots.

Continue along the path upstream for about 800m (875yd), then turn right along Watery Lane (which often lives up to its name). When you reach a cattle grid after 1.25km (¾ mile), turn left, cross the stream and ascend Winsford Hill.

3 Winsford Hill

Your climb will be repaid by the excellent views of patchwork fields as

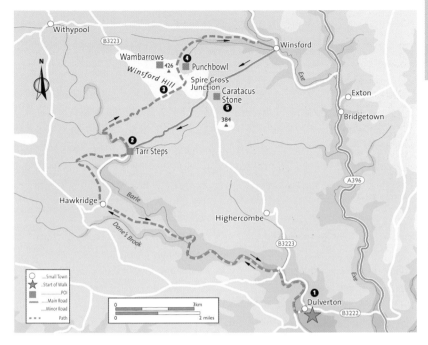

well as three Bronze Age burial mounds called the Wambarrows. Exmoor ponies are among the many species that frequent this area. Winsford, at the bottom of the other side of the hill, is a beautiful spot for a pub lunch.

Take one of the grassy tracks going east, which descend rapidly, to a large hollow that looks similar to an amphitheatre.

4 Punchbowl

Punchbowl is another of the devil's contributions to Exmoor. He is said to have created this depression when making Dunkery Beacon, the highest hill on the moor.

Staying to the east side of the B3223, follow a footpath from the Punchbowl, down through farmland into Winsford.

Make a sharp turn right onto an unnumbered road and follow it until you reach the Spire Cross Junction, site of the Caratacus Stone (slightly obscured by foliage).

5 Caratacus Stone

Dating, it is thought, from the Bronze Age, this monument is inscribed in Latin. The odd-looking shelter that protects it is 100 years old itself.

Keep going south for about 1.5km (1 mile), then cross the cattle grid on the Tarr Steps Road and pick up the footpath which will return you to the river crossing, and Dulverton should you wish. You can also walk back to Dulverton by following the B3223 southeast for 10km (6 miles).

The Beast of Bodmin

Mysterious big cats prowling the wilds of Britain are not exclusive to Bodmin. Phantom felines have stalked areas up and down the land from Cornwall to the Cotswolds and from Trellech to Telford. Hoax and hysteria have undoubtedly played a part in stoking the myth, and the eerie environs of Bodmin are the ideal backdrop for such a story to capture the public imagination. Add a government inquiry and denial and an iconic photo and a legend is created.

Reports of a large, panther-like creature in the area began to surface in the early 1980s. Occasional mutilations of livestock were followed by 'sightings' of the beast. Numerous theories abounded. A popular one was that big cats were being secretly imported for zoos or private collections. The illegality of doing so would have precluded those involved from reporting it to the police, should an animal have escaped. Another was that the animals were members of a species of wildcat wrongly assumed to have become extinct in the 1870s. Experts concluded that Bodmin and its surrounds were home to a population of large cats, although the more compelling idea of a lone creature patrolling the moor gained traction, ensuring the Beast of Bodmin was never pluralised.

The public clamour for answers grew, but a government inquiry in 1995 found no evidence of big cats. Just one week after the conclusion was announced, however, a new furore erupted when a 14-year-old boy walking along the River Fowey happened upon the jawless skull of a large feline. Examination of the object by experts at the Natural History Museum revealed it to be a genuine leopard skull – albeit one that had been imported as part of a leopard-skin rug. But the hoax did nothing to quash the speculation. Three years later the British press amassed at Newquay Zoo, where a grainy video purported to show two panther-like cats prowling around the Jamaica Inn area. A blurred still from the film, depicting one of the creatures staring straight into the lens, became the unofficial face of the beast. The view that the animal was just a large domestic cat failed to dent credence, as did other subsequent suggested explanations for sightings: big dog, small pony, wild boar.

Searches were stepped up. In 1999, a squadron of Cornish RAF reserves used military night-vision equipment to hunt the beast, unsuccessfully. The MP for North Cornwall called for another inquiry, claiming that witnesses 'did not take kindly to being portrayed as gullible yokels, deluded by a trick of the light or an alcoholic haze. After that, they naturally kept their information to themselves.' Dozens of sightings have been recorded since the early 1980s, and the myth lives on, sustained by several references in popular culture, from the cult horror film *Dog Soldiers* and title of a Cornish comedian's video to a VISA advert shot in New Zealand. The difficulty of proving a negative – that no big cat stalks the moors – and the human fascination with mysterious beasts and bogeymen that feeds such myths as the Loch Ness Monster and Bigfoot look set to keep the Beast of Bodmin alive for some time.

The Beast of Bodmin, by sculptor Kate Denton, one of the many artists who have drawn inspiration from the myth

When to go

By British standards, Devon and Cornwall enjoy some excellent weather, with average temperatures the highest in the country. However, the key phrase here is 'by British standards' – the climate in this corner of southwest England can be capricious, with teeming rain quickly seeing off glorious sunshine. A coastal destination, here the wind is sometimes ferocious. While July and August promise the best weather, this is no secret: the summer months bring tourists in droves.

Because many of the region's highlights are outdoors, weather will certainly be a factor in the timing of your trip. Coastal walks, beaches and scenic points like Land's End rapidly lose their allure when you're rain-lashed, windswept and freezing. Some accommodation closes for the winter, and the attractions typically have limited opening hours or may shut their doors entirely for the low season (usually from October to Easter). Public transport is also reduced in winter, which can be a big factor if you're not bringing your own vehicle.

At the other end of the scale is summer, when the best and most reliable weather (again, by British standards) sees Devon and Cornwall packed out. The school holidays (end of July and August) are peak season, with British families heading en masse to the region. Besides the obvious extra queues and traffic, this also pushes up accommodation prices and reduces availability. Exceptional rooms (family suites, for example) in highly sought-after hotels can be booked several years in advance for the school holidays, and even if you're just after a run-of-the-

A common sight on Dartmoor

mill room it's wise to plan ahead. Some hotels may insist on a minimum length of stay.

Other busy periods include Easter, which again sees an influx of families, and, to a lesser extent, every weekend outside the depths of winter. More localised spikes in demand can occur at popular festivals and in pheasant-shooting season. While some establishments, particularly of the small, family-run kind, choose Christmas and New Year to shut up shop, demand for those that do remain open can be relatively high.

Aesthetically, Devon and Cornwall's marvellous countryside and rustic villages clearly benefit from blue skies, which are more likely in summer. Spring and autumn both have a lot to recommend them, as the foliage first blooms beautifully then turns and falls. Although the weather is not quite as clement during these times as it is in peak season, you should still get a few sunny days.

Taking cost, crowds and climate into consideration, travellers with the luxury of some leeway over the timing of their trip would be best off plumping for a warmish time outside the main holiday season. Travel between the end of the Easter holiday and mid-July, or from mid-September to October, and you'll avoid the worst excesses of the summer season without compromising too much on the weather. Of course, if you're going with the children, you won't have much choice; in which case budget extra and book as far ahead as you can.

WEATHER CONVERSION CHART

25.4mm = 1 inch
$^\circ F = 1.8 \times {}^\circ C + 32$

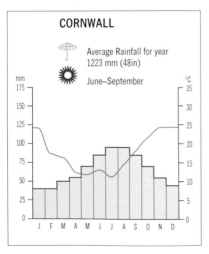

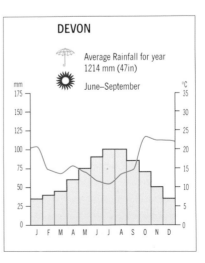

Getting around

If you're planning to visit a few different towns on your trip, particularly some of the more isolated ones in the national parks, a car really comes in handy. You might not think so when you're sitting in holiday traffic, but attempt to navigate the decent but intermittent (and not cheap) public transport network and you'll find yourself longing for the convenience. For scenic journeys, there are super plane, train and boat trips.

By train

If you're sticking largely to the major cities, the train network will suffice. Trains from Exeter go to Plymouth, Truro and Penzance, among other, smaller stations. Journey time from Exeter to Penzance is around three hours and costs from about £16 for a one-way ticket. Branch lines – such as the Tarka Line from Exeter to Barnstaple, the Looe Valley Line, which goes to Liskeard, and the St Ives Bay Line connecting with St Erth – often make for picturesque journeys, taking in the coast or national parkland. Private operators have seized on the aesthetic potential of rail travel, and you will also find some of the old lines (from the regional railway's Victorian heyday) restored and run as tourist attractions in season.

If rail travel will feature heavily in your itinerary, it's worth investigating the so-called 'rover' passes, which allow a certain number of days' travel over a longer period of time. Separate day rovers for Devon and Cornwall are also available, as are tickets which combine rail and bus journeys. Trains generally have good disabled access. It is sometimes better to call ahead, but if you turn up on spec, information about how to get help is often on display in the station.

www.nationalrail.co.uk covers the whole country, providing details of times, fares, and so on, and *www.cornwallpublictransport.info* gives details of public transport throughout Cornwall.

By bus

Buses can be useful for reaching the out-of-the-way places not on the train network, although you will have to plan carefully: smaller towns and villages may see just one bus service daily, or indeed fewer. As with the train, there is a selection of passes, on sale in travel agents and tourist offices as well as from the driver, which will be more cost-effective if you're going to make frequent journeys. Bus travel is generally cheaper than going by train. Some buses, but by no means all, are wheelchair-accessible. The situation is better in larger towns and cities than the villages.

Bus services are provided by various companies, but *www.travelinesw.com* has information on all public transport options in the southwest.

By car

If you're touring the region, the car cannot be beaten for convenience. Having your own vehicle frees you from the rather restrictive train network and bus timetable and allows you to pitch up in small hamlets and remote national park villages at your leisure. With the high cost of public transport in the UK, a group in particular would certainly save money by driving. The main drawback of being car-bound is the traffic, which in peak season can be a big frustration, with caravans and camper vans clogging up the road. Parking can also be a bane, particularly in the busy but tiny holiday villages.

The main roads that bisect the region and the average streets are in excellent condition, but venturing into the villages is another matter. Narrow country roads are the norm in some parts, necessitating intricate reversing manoeuvres that are often contingent on your fellow drivers' courtesy. Fortunately, most motorists are fairly pleasant and cooperative about the

whole business. One car usually has to shunt backwards to the nearest recess, labelled passing place (usually with the 'p' removed by local wags!), allowing the other to pass. 'Thank you' and 'you're welcome' waves are then liberally exchanged. Things are further complicated by the large hedgerows that sometimes line the lanes and decrease visibility. If you're heading for remoter locales, keep an eye on your petrol gauge to avoid getting stuck on a dark lane in the middle of nowhere. In the UK, cars drive on the left.

Car hire and taxis

Renting a car is perfectly possible in Devon and Cornwall, with Exeter the main centre for car hire outlets such as

Rail journeys around the peninsula are often scenic

Hertz (*www.hertz.co.uk*) and **Budget**
(*www.budget.co.uk*), among others.
Taxis, some of which are adapted to
take wheelchairs, can be a useful but
costly way to reach the further-flung
environs or get back to your hotel after
the last bus.

By boat

Although, with the exception of
voyages to the Isles of Scilly and
Lundy, you can pass your entire trip
without stepping off dry land, ferries
can make a scenic alternative to road
travel in Devon and Cornwall. Given
the influence that seafaring has exerted
on the counties over the centuries, it
would be a shame not to take to the
waves at least once, weather
permitting. In some cases, the sea
route can be more efficient, for
example where an estuary forces the
coast road inland and then out again
to reach the next town. Dartmouth to
Kingswear and Falmouth to St Mawes
are among the wealth of possible ferry
trips (*see www.cornwall.gov.uk*).
Demand, of course, rises significantly
in peak season, which can make
summer ferry journeys a protracted
experience. Some ferries take foot
passengers only.

One of the most important boat
journeys is to the Isles of Scilly. The

Driving can be a great way of getting away from it all

two-hour 40-minute journey is for foot passengers only (unless there are exceptional circumstances). The service runs between Easter and October, once or twice per day, with the exception of Sunday. Details including prices, which start at £80 for an adult return, with children travelling half-price, are available on the website of the company that operates both the ferry and plane, **Isles of Scilly Travel** (*www.islesofscilly-travel.co.uk*). A visit to Lundy Island (*www.lundyisland.co.uk*) also necessitates a boat trip. The two-hour journey costs less than half as much as to Scilly, and runs from April to October.

By plane

Both Scilly and Lundy are also reachable by air, the former by plane and helicopter (*www.islesofscilly-travel.co.uk*) and the latter by chopper (*www.lundyisland.co.uk*) from November to March.

By bike

If you have the stamina, cycling is a splendid way to avoid most of the traffic snarl-ups while taking in the spectacular scenery. Various scenic and coastal routes can be done by bike, and the National Cycle Network also passes through the region. Hire outlets can be found on the main cycling trails. The region's eco-philosophy certainly encourages cyclists, who, for example, get discounted entry to the Eden Project. You can download the 2010 National Cycle Network map at

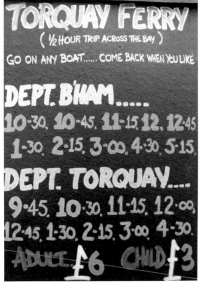

With the sea such an important part of the region, it would be a shame not to take to the water

www.sustrans.org.uk. Routes can also be downloaded from *www.visitcornwall.com* and *www.devon.gov.uk*. Some visitors' centres and bicycle rental outlets may also be able to help.

On foot

Hiking is another wonderful way to see the counties, with the 1,014km (630-mile) South West Coast Path just the most famous of many rewarding trails (*www.southwestcoastpath.com*). Walking will also suffice in the towns, with even the larger conurbations, such as Plymouth and Exeter, having compact enough centres to render cars and public transport largely unnecessary.

Accommodation

All kinds of accommodation can be found throughout Devon and Cornwall, from grand hotels to homely B&Bs and no-frills campsites. At the top end are some splendid, characterful boutique hotels, whose design and service are so superb they rival the best in Britain. On the other hand, the climate lends itself to camping, and you can't drive for long without coming across the brown road sign with the tent and caravan.

The region's well-developed tourist industry means that in the most popular destinations there is a plethora of different places to stay, to suit every wallet. Naturally, your options are more limited in the villages, where the main accommodation is in the shape of informal B&Bs. As well as campsites aplenty, cheaper facilities include youth hostels, university accommodation, and camping barns and bunkhouses, which dot the main hiking and cycling trails.

B&Bs and guesthouses

Less standardised than hotels, B&Bs ('bed and breakfasts') and guesthouses provide informal accommodation, often at great value. A sign outside sometimes communicates to passers-by vacancies, or lack thereof. The personal touch often plays a big part in the charm of the place, although some can be quite large and professional. Bathrooms are often, but not always, shared. Prices start from about £40 for

a double (the financial crisis may have driven some even lower), with more upmarket ones costing as much as low- to mid-range hotels. Bear in mind that the owners may not have credit card facilities. Local tourist offices often have lists of approved places, or you can try the following:
www.bedbreakfastcornwall.com
www.cornishlight.co.uk
www.devonfarms.co.uk
www.devon-online.com

Camping

The region is chock-full of campsites, and in some places you can even pitch your tent on the moor. Facilities again differ significantly, with prices starting from about £5 for a two-person tent.
www.caravancampingsites.co.uk
www.devon-connect.co.uk

Hiker accommodation

Catering for the cyclists and hikers who flock to the counties, basic accommodation in largely rural

locations is another option for budget travellers in Devon and Cornwall. It falls into two kinds: bunkhouses and camping barns. The former, some of which are YHA-affiliated, consist of dormitory accommodation with bathroom (offering hot water) and kitchen. Many also have private rooms sleeping four. You will need your own sleeping bag. Expect to pay around £10. Bunkhouses are more comfortable and better equipped than camping barns. These come with sleeping platforms and a basic food preparation area. You'll have a flush toilet but no hot water. Camping barns can be either booked for your sole use (indeed, if you're travelling with young children in tow this can be obligatory) or shared with other travellers. You'll pay from £6 up, and will need to bring your own utensils, camping stove, etc.
www.yha.org.uk

Holiday cottages

Rental accommodation, in the form of city flats or, more commonly, holiday cottages, can offer excellent value, in particular if you're travelling in a group or if you book at the last minute when the owner is keen not to lose the revenue. Not only do the prices compare favourably to hotel rates, but such a venue affords you a great deal of freedom: no set breakfast hours, no staff or guests to be polite to, you can make your own dinner when you please and also wander around in your pyjamas should the mood take you.

Cottages usually sleep around four to six people, but you can also find larger and smaller ones, and some come with the option of camp or sofa beds for extra flexibility. Prices – rental is usually per week – vary considerably: the cheapest place may be the right side of £200 in winter or early spring, with large, sought-after seafront properties commanding well over £1,000 in high season. The large disparity in price reflects the location and standards: while some are well placed and boast impressive amenities, others may be cold, poky and in the middle of nowhere. Kitchens usually come with a decent complement of crockery and cookware, and bed sheets and towels are also generally provided.
www.classic.co.uk
www.nationaltrustcottages.co.uk
www.southwestholidaycottages.com

Traditional English décor is popular in old inns

Accommodation

Hotels

The best hotels in Devon and Cornwall come with ocean, river or moor views, superlative service, Egyptian cotton bed sheets, chocolates on pillows and marvellous breakfast spreads. It would be quite easy to spend £200 or upwards on one of the high-end choices. Even at the low end, you're unlikely to get away with paying much less than £60 a night for a double room.

Some of the more special establishments are housed in buildings that date back hundreds of years, with tasteful touches bringing them into the 21st century. You may find yourself spending a few days in a former abbey, corn mill, farmhouse, barn – even a railway carriage. The traditional style adopted by many hotels means that non-British visitors should expect to come into contact with the separate

hot and cold taps that bewilder many foreigners, along with other similar eccentricities. Restrictions on adaptations to listed buildings mean that some owners have had to be inventive to convert the property into a hotel and you may find quirks such as tiny bathrooms in converted cupboards. Hotels almost always include breakfast in the room rate. The following sites provide information on hotels as well as other types of accommodation:
www.cornwall-online.co.uk
www.devonhotels.com
www.visitcornwall.com

Inns

Some of the region's more distinctive accommodation is found in inns, or country pubs. With buildings dating back centuries, such properties are steeped in history and can make a very atmospheric place to stay. As well as a typically low number of rooms, the venue will also contain one or more bars, often popular with the local townspeople, and usually a restaurant too. Some of the latter aspire to and reach very high standards. Many such places can be found in the smaller towns inside the national parks. Depending on the level of luxury the owners have implemented, you can pay as little as you would at a B&B, or as much as for a good hotel. For information, check hotel websites and the following:
www.iknow-devon.co.uk

Fowey's Old Quay House updates a historical location with 21st-century boutique style

A nautical-inspired bedroom at Tresanton

University accommodation

The exodus of students over the summer months frees up much of the region's university lets, which some institutions then hire out to travellers. Prices are comparable with youth hostel costs, although can go higher. Conditions are unlikely to be particularly luxurious, but the location can be conveniently close to the centre of town. Some private and en-suite rooms are available.

www.exeter.ac.uk

Youth hostels

Devon and Cornwall have a network of youth hostels, both registered Youth Hostel Association properties and independent ones. If you're travelling solo and hoping to meet like-minded people, or if you're on a budget, hostels can be an excellent resource. Most enjoy enviable locations, either in the city centre or close to major places of interest. Many now offer high-standard facilities, including private rooms, and some are branching out into novelty accommodation such as Nordic Tipis. Because they have to stick to regulations, YHA places can have more of an institutional feel, while the absence of such regulations governing independent hostels can make them more hit-and-miss. A night's kip starts at around £12 in low season, rising to around £20 when demand is highest. Membership gets you discounted accommodation at YHA facilities so can be worth investing in if you're planning to stay more than a few nights. Non-YHA places sometimes have mixed dorms.

www.yha.org.uk

Food and drink

While British cuisine in general is, perhaps unfairly, maligned, gastronomy is likely to be a big part of your trip to the region. Days start with scrumptious hotel breakfasts, and the miles of coastline bring a wealth of fresh seafood to your plate. Cornwall is becoming something of a celebrity restaurant mecca, pioneered by Jamie Oliver and Rick Stein. And the Cornish pasty and Devon cream tea are two calorific classics you shouldn't miss.

While fish obviously features heavily, and the hunting traditions in parts of the counties have popularised game, switched-on hoteliers and restaurateurs always make sure vegetarians are catered for.

Local cuisine

It's been a long time since a *New York Times* food critic wrote 'Cornwall, England probably offers more bad food per square mile than anywhere else in the civilised world'. The geography of Devon and Cornwall is one of the reasons behind their superlative cuisine. Primarily, there's the fish. When your hotel or restaurant is right on the seafront, freshness – and therefore taste – reaches new heights. Fishing is integral to the history and economy of southwest England, with pretty trawlers dotting the coast and other evidence of the industry all around, so by ordering seafood you're imbibing the atmosphere and traditions as much as consuming the meal itself. In total, over 40 species of seafood are caught off the peninsula, including sole, monkfish, mackerel and sea bass, not to mention oysters, crab and lobster.

But it's not just sheer weight of numbers that contributes to the thriving fishing industry and gastronomic delights. The region's tourism entrepreneurs know exactly what their customers want, and take

A SOVEREIGN SUPPORTER

Perhaps the most famous proponent of organic produce associated with the region is Prince Charles. Famous for talking to his plants, the future king of England, one of whose titles is Duke of Cornwall, has been a supporter of organic farming for over two decades, starting long before it became fashionable. Established in 1337, the Duchy of Cornwall, a private estate of almost 55,000 hectares (135,900 acres) of land, mostly in southwest England, produces various items, from biscuits to body lotion, employing eco-friendly principles. The county hosted the first factory dedicated to producing the prince's food brand Duchy Originals.

steps to cook the day's catch in the most original and mouthwatering ways. Restaurants showcase their seafood superbly, and often have a day's fish special.

The coastline may make fish the most obvious gastronomic highlight, but it is far from the only one. Devon and Cornwall are also rich in farmland, and the former is spearheading the UK's organic food vanguard, with the most organic farms and land in the country. Top-quality dairy products including a plethora of tasty cheeses, vegetables and meat can be enjoyed with no guilt over food miles, and increasing numbers of local restaurateurs are seizing the eco zeitgeist and flagging up their local sourcing of products, sometimes down to specifying the name of their supplier on the menu. This all translates into quite delicious meals.

Specialities

The staple of Cornish cuisine is the famed pasty. This semicircular savoury pie has a filling of meat chunks, potato and onion, which bake in the pastry casing. (*Its legendary status merits a section of its own, and the pasty is explored in its full glory on*

Scrumptious: ciders and ales have a fervent local following

Food and drink

pp138–9.) Devon's equivalent standard bearer is its cream tea (*see box*), while locally made ice cream is another treat.

Drinks

This part of the world is synonymous with cider, or scrumpy as it is known in southwest England, from 'scrump', the local dialect term for a withered apple. Devon is particularly associated with cider production, but not always happily so. In the 17th century, lead poisoning suffered by cider drinkers in the county gave rise to a condition labelled Devon colic, which could occasionally be fatal. But the affliction did not dent the locals' enthusiasm for the beverage, which remains the county's traditional drink. In keeping with the region's olde-worlde traditions, real ales are also popular. The most famous is St Austell, brewed locally for over a century and a half. But other, smaller establishments also produce brews, such as Dartmoor's

The quintessentially English cream tea

DEVON CREAM TEA

Consisting of scones (biscuit-like quick breads made of oatmeal, wheat flour, barley meal or similar), with butter, jam and a large dollop of Devon clotted cream, accompanied by a pot of tea, this traditional snack is served in cafés and hotels from mid-afternoon, although the hospitality industry has adapted to the on-demand age and it can now usually be found throughout the day. Clotted Devonshire cream is believed by historians to have first been enjoyed by the villagers of Tavistock, given by way of thanks from the Benedictine monks whose abbey the people were helping to repair. This timing means the Devon cream tea probably celebrated a millennium of existence around 2005.

quirky Jail Ale. Climatic conditions have allowed a burgeoning viticulture, and demand is high for many local wines. The other famous local tipple is Plymouth Gin, an EU-protected trademark.

Where to eat

The counties offer a wealth of places to eat, from simple cafés to fabulous restaurants from which you will emerge, full to bursting, after several hours. Hotels also play a significant role in the local gastronomic scene, their restaurants popular with residents and locals alike. As well as the obvious chains, the area has a wonderful array of independent cafés, where the fare is sandwiches, salads, jacket potatoes with fillings, cakes, coffees, teas and soft drinks. Restaurants run the gamut from simple eateries up to the celebrity venues of Jamie Oliver and Rick Stein,

Products piscatorial are Padstow's lifeblood

as well as Michelin-starred marvels. Pubs and inns serve simpler fare, but may have their own posh restaurant too. Top tourist attractions usually have cafés, or at least stalls where you can get a bite to eat.

Meal times

Hotel breakfasts are generally served from 7 or 8 to 9 or 10am. While in the larger towns it's possible to eat whenever the urge takes you, the villages are more provincial, and mealtimes are more restricted, from about noon to 2pm for lunch and 6 to 9 or 10pm for dinner. Cafés are usually open by 10am, if not earlier, and stay open until around 6pm.

Where to buy food

Markets and the souvenir shops of the major attractions often stock a wide range of local food and drink products.

Costs

Eating in the region is not cheap. A lunch, consisting of sandwich, coffee and cake, say, in a café will seldom cost less than £10, while a two-course restaurant meal with wine starts from around £15 and could reach five times the amount.

The Cornish pasty

Few things symbolise Cornwall as much as the pasty. With a history dating back hundreds (some say thousands) of years, it started life as a humble convenience food for miners and has grown into a multi-million-pound industry with offshoots all over the world. Like many cherished icons, it has also generated more than its fair share of controversy.

Although nothing is known definitively about the earliest Cornish pasties, historians believe the snack developed as sustenance for the county's tin miners, who had to take their food with them and eat it underground. Held next to the body, the pasty's heat-retention capacity helped keep the carrier warm. Portability was important, as was identification: pasties were baked with the purchaser's initials imprinted in the pastry, so there could be no confusing half-eaten ones underground. With no hand-washing facilities, miners had to be careful not to inadvertently consume any arsenic from the tin. The pasty could be gripped by the folded crust, which could then be discarded – a practice also said to have some superstitious grounds. Cast-off pasty ends were thought to appease the 'Knockers', mischievous subterranean spirits. Some even argue that the food long predates its supposed origins. The author of *The Official Encyclopaedia of the Cornish Pasty* believes it could be as much as 10,000 years old.

The fame of the Cornish pasty travelled wide. Shakespeare puts it in no fewer than three of his plays, including the inventive simile 'if ye pinch me like a pasty, I can say no more' in *All's Well That Ends Well*. Rather more gruesomely, in *Titus Andronicus* the protagonist bakes two of his enemies' bodies into a pasty which he force-feeds to their mother. Chaucer's *The Canterbury Tales* name-checks the pasty twice, and it also pops up in a range of books, songs and films from medieval times to today. Pasties have won well-connected fans: a letter has been found from a baker to Henry VIII's third wife Jane Seymour, in which he writes that he hopes 'this pasty reaches in better condition than the last one'.

With such publicity and devotion, it is hardly surprising that a fondness for the pasty spread around the world. Emigrating miners took their dietary habits with them. Churches in slate-belt mining regions of eastern Pennsylvania still hold 'pastie suppers', and Michigan hosts an annual Pasty Fest (Finnish immigrants to the state also adopted the snack as their own). Other US states, Mexico, Australia and Sri Lanka also saw significant Cornish migration and a resulting reverence for the food. But one place the pasty did not manage to conquer was the water: local superstition held it as bad luck for a fisherman to take one out to sea with him.

Where there is success, there is often dispute. The discovery of a pasty recipe in a 16th-century audit book led to a rival claim from Devon as the place to have given birth to the famous fare. And not everyone sees the pasty as an unalloyed good. A US food writer's criticism of the pasty in 1999 ('At least with a hamburger, you can disguise it with relish, but with a pasty, you've got this five-pound football-shape thing sitting in your hand and there's nothing you can do with it') prompted pasty shop owner Ann Muller to burn an American flag in protest at the iconoclasm.

The humble pasty has gone from miner's convenience food to culinary Cornish icon

Entertainment

Devon and Cornwall offer the visitor myriad ways to keep occupied. Some of the most enjoyable are connected to the outdoors, such as the Eden Project, the national parks and Land's End. But the inside attractions are also well worth your time. A flourishing arts scene can be found in St Ives, Falmouth, Newlyn and Exeter. And quaint old pubs, charming cafés and top contemporary restaurants will also compete for your time.

It's not difficult to find out what's going on in the area. Big events are listed in local newspapers, and the plethora of magazines (from posh glossies to simple newsletter-type sheets) found in tourist offices, local attractions and hotels give detailed listings. Large venues, such as theatres, almost always have websites, if you want to check in advance what productions coincide with your visit, and posters and information are usually displayed in the window. Various arts centres throughout the region also serve as hubs, advertising events in the area. At places such as the Phoenix Arts Centre in Exeter, for example, you can pick up an enormous array of leaflets and listings guides to the local area, and staff will also be happy to point you in the right direction.

In general, the arts scene is most lively in places with either large student populations, such as Exeter and Falmouth, or towns that have previously been nuclei of the arts, such as St Ives. The former are your best bet for informal entertainment such as live music and comedy nights, the latter for official events such as retrospectives and exhibitions. The cities and larger towns all have a fine selection of restaurants, but any location that welcomes significant numbers of tourists will have at least a handful of good places to eat.

THE PIRATES OF PENZANCE

With its plot hinging on a mishearing (a maid understands that her employer wishes his son apprenticed to a pirate, rather than a ship's pilot), comic opera *The Pirates of Penzance* is one of Gilbert and Sullivan's most popular works. Two jokes are contained in the title. One is the unlikelihood of pirates in a genteel resort such as Penzance. The second is a dig at the creative piracy that saw the duo's *HMS Pinafore* ripped off in the USA. *Pirates'* cultural impact was such that allusions to it appear everywhere from *The Simpsons* to *Grand Theft Auto*, and The Major-General's Song has been satirised ad infinitum.

Tourist attractions

One of the UK's top holiday destinations, many of the counties' best attractions are familiar names. Land's End, the westernmost point of the mainland UK, is a must-see for most visitors, with posing for a photo next to the iconic signpost (indicating New York 3,147 miles in one direction and John O'Groats 874 in the other) the southwest's equivalent of pretending to support the Leaning Tower of Pisa. But while Land's End and the environmental complex of the Eden Project are the big guns, the region is home to a multitude of lesser-known, quirky gems such as the delightful Museum of Witchcraft in Boscastle, where dedication and imagination make up for the absence of celebrity.

Arts centres

Cornwall in particular has thriving arts hubs, which serve as useful ports of call. As well as being able to provide visitors with information on the local arts scene, venues such as Exeter's Phoenix host a range of cultural events, from films, dance, music and drama to workshops and exhibitions. Some galleries in the region, the most famous of which is the local outpost of the Tate at St Ives, have also branched out into events, such as talks, performances and workshops.

Pubs

Anyone visiting Devon and Cornwall from outside the UK will find the local pubs an endearing part of British culture. Even if you're familiar

Local pubs offer a down-to-earth dining experience, plus plenty of ale to help wash down your meal

with the concept, the rustic style of most of the region's drinking holes (think low roofs, original wooden beams, resident dogs and the odd stuffed animal to celebrate the local hunters' prowess) makes them quaint stop-offs. Many, if not most, of the pubs also serve food. This, and the now UK-wide ban on smoking in public places, makes them more appealing to families than they used to be, although some pubs do impose an age limit on children, or ban them altogether.

Cinema

The region has a good selection of cinemas, many showing Hollywood and mainstream pictures, and a few going for artier, alternative titles.

Theatre

Most of the larger towns in Devon and Cornwall have at least one theatre, and some have achieved an impressively high profile. The Theatre Royal Plymouth is one of the most financially successful venues in the UK, up there with

The Barnfield Theatre in Exeter stages comedy, drama, dance and music

the top London playhouses. The open-air Minack is surely the most extraordinary venue, its cliff-side location giving productions a dramatically oceanic background.

Opera, ballet and classical music

The many entertainment venues around Devon and Cornwall typically host a wide range of productions, including opera, ballet, musicals and classical concerts as well as the usual complement of plays. There are also local troupes, both professional and semi-professional, who take their productions predominantly around the region. Both venues and companies have websites advertising their programme. The region's most famous operatic association is Gilbert and Sullivan's

Exeter is a hub of the region's thriving cultural scene

operetta *The Pirates of Penzance*, although the librettist and composer both hailed from London and had only tenuous links with the area (Sullivan composed the music for *Iolanthe* at Pencarrow House in Bodmin).

Folk and other live music

If you're lucky, you may not have to seek out folk music; it will come to you. Amateur performers sometimes pitch up with their instruments at the local pub, and customers are then in for an amiable afternoon listening to their lilting, Celtic-influenced songs. At the other end of the scale, the Cornish Folk Festival (or Wadebridge Folk Festival, as it has now been rebadged) takes place annually. Other live music can be found around the region, particularly in towns with large student populations.

THE MINACK

Like many great ideas, the Minack evolved quite by chance. In the 1920s it was the residence of Rowena Cade, the daughter of a Derbyshire cotton miller. She purchased the Minack (meaning 'rocky') headland for herself and her mother for £100, and they had a house built. In 1929, a local troupe staged *A Midsummer Night's Dream* in a nearby field, and announced that their next production would be *The Tempest*. Thinking the sea would make an appropriate backdrop, Cade offered the players her garden as a venue. Her invitation taken up, she and her gardener fashioned a terrace and rough seating from material they found in the house or on the beach. Following the successful show, Cade spent much of the rest of her life improving the theatre. Minack's 75th anniversary was marked with another production of *The Tempest*.

Shopping

Souvenirs from your trip to the southwest are quite likely to take an edible form. Devon's famous clotted cream, as well as being a rather nice product to take home as it is, is fashioned into other tempting purchases, such as fudge, which make convenient gifts. The region's many organic farms also yield a variety of portable foodstuffs. Arts and crafts are also plentiful, and paintings of coastal scenes can be a charming memento of your stay.

There's almost no limit to the different produce you can take home. The only southwest staple that would defy transportation is the ice cream. Much of what's good comes in jars. Chutney, honey, mustard, jam and other preserves are on sale far and wide. Another quintessentially regional gift would be cider (often styled as 'cyder' for that touch of faux-tradition), or alternatively apple juice for teetotallers and children. Cheeses are a good option, provided they don't have to be carried too great a distance. And there are also the other cream derivative products such as confectionery.

One aspect that makes Devon and Cornwall's edible goodies such good gifts is the presentation. Canny producers have realised that as well as *being* healthy and wholesome, their wares must *look* healthy and wholesome. To this end, tremendous effort has been put into packaging the products, with designers enthusiastically embracing 'farmhouse chic', a professional and slick version of how authentic farm produce would look (think doily-style covers over the jar lid and olde-worlde fonts).

Aside from consumables, the other main genre of souvenirs is arts and crafts. As everywhere, the unfathomable majesty of the sea has drawn artists to

Foodstuffs and seaside paraphernalia are popular purchases

Markets, both farmers' and pannier, make great places to stock up on edible goodies

attempt to capture it on canvas, and generations of painters and craftspeople have made the region their home. Many businesses attempt to boost the trade, and hotels often display (and sell) the work of a local artist in their restaurant and rooms. From time to time you might come across an artist's workshop, where the works are both created and sold. The region is also home to the standard kind of art shops, particularly in the better-known towns of the local arts scene.

Of course, you will also find the usual array of tourist souvenirs. T-shirts, caps, mugs, towels, pens, soft toys and their (often uninspiring) like are generally omnipresent in most shops geared towards holidaymakers. The region's stunning scenery makes calendars and coffee-table books more tempting. You may also find a few

'comedy' souvenirs, such as 'Cornishmen do it dreckly' (meaning later) car stickers.

Where to buy

All of the important tourist attractions have well-stocked shops. The huge emporium at the Eden Project is particularly impressive, selling everything from hammocks to hampers, bulbs to bags, candles to cards and cider to stationery. Naturally, such venues are not the cheapest places to do your shopping. Markets and normal stores usually offer a selection of the same sort of stuff at lower prices, with Devon's pannier markets particularly good for cut-price holiday shopping, as well as for a range of more mundane items. The many farmers' markets are also a good spot to pick up edible items.

Sport and leisure

Wide-open spaces, beaches and clement weather fill Devon and Cornwall with opportunities for outdoor fun. Coastal paths and national parks attract hikers, bikers and horse riders, while the ocean waves give the region some of the UK's best surfing, with other watersports like sailing, canoeing and diving also popular. Meanwhile, the rise of luxury tourism is now introducing a few luxury spas to the area.

Cycling

Stunning scenery, a varied landscape and absence of traffic on many routes give Devon and Cornwall some of the best cycling in the UK. Country lanes, quaint villages and challenging off-road routes are all part of the mix for the bike-bound visitor. There is something for everyone, no matter what your proficiency. The North Cornwall coastal road and its tough gradients – some of the steepest in the land – are a magnet for serious cyclists, and there are other lengthy trails, such as the 164km (102-mile) Devon Coast to Coast route, and the West Country Way, which runs from Bristol to Padstow. Even the novice will be fine on the Camel Trail, which runs along a disused railway line. The national parks also cater to cyclists, with well-marked tracks, graded off-road routes and various maps.

If biking is the main purpose of your trip, specialised tour operators can help you build a tailor-made cycling holiday. Though not dedicated specifically to the region, **Sustrans** (*www.sustrans.org.uk*), a section of Sustainable Transport, can provide information on cycling in general as well as specific routes. The national park and moor authorities may also be of help. If the idea of cycling only grasps you after you've arrived, there are plenty of rental places.

Hiking

The pinnacle of hiking in the region must be the **South West Coast Path**. The 1,014km (630-mile) trail runs along the coast from Minehead in Somerset to Poole Harbour in Dorset, and is the longest path of its kind in Britain. It's suitable for walkers of any ability or energy level – idle visitors can have a half-hour wander, take some photos and then turn back, while dedicated hikers might devote their trip to doing the whole thing. Whatever your inclination, the official website (*www.southwestcoastpath.com*) offers possible routes as well as up-to-date information such as on any closed sections.

Wild and rugged **Dartmoor National Park** is another top spot for walkers. Again, various routes cater to hikers of various appetites, with short guided tours as possible as longer treks over the course of several days. More information is available from the Dartmoor National Park Authority (*www.dartmoor-npa.gov.uk*). Although not as big, **Exmoor**, the region's other national park, has its coastline to recommend it. Again, the Exmoor National Park Authority (*www.exmoor-nationalpark.gov.uk*) runs guided walks and can advise on longer trails, one of which covers 188km (117 miles) and takes about a week. It's not a national park, but Bodmin Moor has old villages, historical sites and a mystical atmospheric that also brings in hikers.

Horse riding

Picture the region's national parks, and if it's not untamed countryside that springs to mind it's likely to be pony-trekking. The animals' association with both Dartmoor and Exmoor is almost timeless. Galloping through the unkempt grassland, you may well feel like some kind of Jane Austen character. The bucolic clip-clopping of horses' hooves is also an occasional pleasant background noise in the villages. There are plenty of stables and riding centres where the beginner can take lessons (from around £15 an hour). Some riding centres have jumped on the tourism bandwagon and also provide accommodation for both rider and horse.

The wilds of Dartmoor are beloved of hikers, bikers and horse riders

Spas

If the more active pursuits sound a bit too much like hard work, you could go for the other growth area in Devon and Cornwall tourism: spas. While they are definitely the exception rather than the rule at the moment, there is a trend in the region of new managers taking over tired old hotels and hauling them upmarket with major renovations. In the attempt to distinguish themselves from their competitors, more could turn to such luxury amenities to tap into the growing popularity of health tourism.

Surfing

Although southwest England lacks the warm climate of more obvious surfing hotspots, such as California or Australia's Gold Coast, Atlantic swells – and thick wetsuits – have facilitated year-round surfing. Ironically, some of the best waves are in wintertime, owing to the low pressure. The action is pretty much all along the north coast of the peninsula. The epicentre of the local surfing scene is Newquay, whose Fistral Beach is arguably the country's most famous. The town's status is probably due in part to its size, meaning that

Surfers come from far and wide to ride the waves of Devon and Cornwall

there's plenty of après-surf socialising after the sun sets on the day's water-based activities. Other hotspots include Croyde, Woolacombe, Saunton, Bantham and Putsborough in Devon, and Bude, Polzeath, Constantine Bay and Sennen Cove in Cornwall.

Because of the difficulty involved in getting started – you're likely to spend significant time just struggling to get and stay on your feet – lessons are strongly recommended. There are various surf schools in the area open all year round. You'll pay from about £30 for half a day's tuition, and hiring the wetsuit will set you back another £10 or so. The **South West Surf** (*www.southwestsurf.info*) website posts a long list of links to other relevant sites, including so-called surfcams, which post up-to-date images of the beach and detail wave conditions, and weather information. If you haven't booked anything in advance, you should be able to find a school simply by wandering around any of the surf towns, particularly Newquay. (*The development of surfing is covered in more detail on pp38–9.*)

Kitesurfing and windsurfing are also popular watersports

Other watersports

Surfing might be the most glamorous, but it's far from the only watersport happening in the region. Kitesurfing seems to be the latest addition to the scene, and windsurfing, while somewhat eclipsed by its sail-free cousin, has the advantage of being possible away from the surf beaches, which can get crowded in summer. Sailing is an alternative, particularly in the summer months. The clear waters also afford splendid visibility for scuba divers. The tragedy of seafarers past is the boon of today's divers: some of the best sites are among the 4,600 old wrecks that lie, forlornly, on the seabed, awaiting exploration. Away from the sea, the region's rivers are home to kayaking and canoeing, both gentle glides downstream and the full-on white-water variety for thrill seekers.

Children

Children will adore Devon and Cornwall. On top of the observable delights of the beach and national parks, many of the big tourist attractions go to pains to entertain their younger clientele. Several of the water-based and adventure sports detailed previously can be enjoyed by older children. But even aside from organised fun, there is plenty of inadvertent amusement to be had, such as watching the fishermen at work or spotting surfers.

Providing the weather is warm enough, the beach will occupy children for a good while, particularly younger ones. Many of the beaches in the area are sandy, although some do have shingles. While the popular places usually have lifeguards in high season, the cover is by no means complete and they tend to leave by 6pm. For further details on this, as well as other useful information like the presence of toilets and things for youngsters to do, the following websites are full of tips: *www.familyholidaysouthwest.co.uk* and *www.easypreschoolsouthwest.co.uk*

The other main outdoor draws are the two national parks, Exmoor and Dartmouth, and Bodmin Moor. Their atmospheric terrain, the many myths associated with them and the abundance of quirky features will excite small visitors – what child would not be enthused by the fabled Beast of Bodmin (*see pp122–3*)? And of course, there is also the practical stuff to do. Older children will enjoy tramping around on short walks, and horse riding will also appeal. Parents seeking some down time can book their brood in for lessons.

The vast majority of tourist attractions for adults will also appeal to children. While Land's End, for example, might be of limited interest to kids on its own, the addition of a child-oriented theme park (including a *Doctor Who* exhibit, featuring a moving Dalek, and the award-winning 4D pirate film, *The Curse of Skull Rock* (*see p89*) will appeal. The Eden Project (*see pp84–5*), with its big biomes and multitude of exhibits, is a fantastic venue to take children, and you could quite easily spend the whole day there. The region's castles are also ripe for exploration, with the King Arthur association making a trip to Tintagel (*see p77*) especially thrilling for young history buffs. Even if your little ones have no interest in history, however, the nooks and crannies are still fun to investigate.

Museums, zoos, aquaria (*see p35 for Ilfracombe Aquarium, p57 for National Marine Aquarium and p64 for Blue Reef Aquarium*) and adventure parks are likely to be another source of entertainment for kids. While some of the first category can be stuffy and off-putting for children, most museums are making an effort to modernise, introducing interactive exhibits and colourful displays. Even in the most unlikely of places there are hidden gems: open an innocuous cupboard in Ilfracombe Museum (*see p35*) to find dozens of 1930s bats preserved in jars. Idiosyncratic museums on themes such as witchcraft and smuggling will also fascinate youngsters. (*See pp74 and 82–3 for the Museum of Witchcraft and National Maritime Museum Cornwall, and for older children Dartmoor Prison Museum (pp115–16) and Jamaica Inn*

(*p117*).) **Woodlands Adventure Park** is set in 90 acres of woodland and includes a zoo, farm, falconry centre with 50 birds of prey and wildlife sanctuary. There are 16 rides for those of a more adventurous bent, and indoor facilities ensure that even if the heavens open the day won't be a washout. Gentler play zones cater to smaller customers. *Blackawton, Totnes. Tel: 01803 712 598. www.woodlandspark.com Open: Easter–early Nov 9.30am–varies, summer holidays 9.30am–6pm. Admission charge.*

Child-friendliness varies. While some hotels and restaurants welcome children, others try to deter families to preserve a more sedate atmosphere. It is certainly worth enquiring ahead. Family-oriented places should have high chairs, children's menus and other conveniences.

Mudlarking on the beach in St Ives

Essentials

Arriving and departing
By bus
Reaching Devon and Cornwall by bus is the cheapest way for lone travellers, with Exeter the main hub. From London Victoria, National Express services leave nine times a day, taking from 4¼ to 5 hours. Birmingham and Bristol also have regular services. Plymouth sees slightly fewer buses, and you can also reach Penzance, Truro, Bodmin, Falmouth and Newquay. Book ahead and travel outside peak times (weekends, summer and Christmas) for the cheapest fares, which can be under £10.

National Express (*www.nationalexpress.com*) runs the most comprehensive service, with competitors like **Megabus** (*www.megabus.com/uk*) operating on major routes.

By train
Quicker and more comfortable than the coach, train travel is usually costlier. About two trains leave London Paddington every hour for Exeter, with direct services taking 2 to 2¼ hours, an hour longer for Plymouth. Penzance has a less frequent 5-hour service from London. A return from London to Exeter starts at around £60; it can be cheaper to buy two singles. Walk-on fares can be extortionate, so try to book at least two weeks in advance and specify the service for the best deals.

www.firstgreatwestern.co.uk
www.thetrainline.com
www.nationalrail.co.uk

By car
The M5 motorway links Birmingham and Exeter, joining up with the M4 from London en route. From the centre of London, the journey time to Exeter is about 3 hours 40 minutes, and the distance under 320km (200 miles). Exeter to Penzance will take you another 2½ hours.

By plane
There are three main airports in the region, in Exeter (*www.exeter-airport.co.uk*), Plymouth (*www.plymouthairport.com*) and Newquay (*www.newquaycornwallairport.com*). Exeter has scheduled flights, largely with Flybe (*www.flybe.com*), to destinations in Britain and mainland Europe. Plymouth Airport has flights to the major domestic and Irish destinations, as does Newquay with the addition of a few services to the continent.

By ferry
Outside winter, visitors from France can take the ferry from Roscoff to Plymouth, with longer, less frequent sailings from Santander in Spain. *www.brittany-ferries.co.uk*

Customs

If you're travelling to the UK from the European Union, you can bring cigarettes and alcohol for personal consumption. Some EU countries impose individual restrictions, so check in advance if in doubt. People arriving from outside the EU can bring in 200 cigarettes or the equivalent, 2l of wine or 1l of spirits, plus other goods worth up to £390. Any more must be declared. *www.hmrc.gov.uk*

Electricity

British plugs are the three flat pin variety, and the electricity supply is 230 volts. Adaptors for foreign appliances are usually on sale in airports and electrical goods stores.

Internet

As well as Internet cafés, you can go online in libraries (often for free) and tourist offices. Many hotels, restaurants and bars have installed wireless access for use with customers' laptops. Connections are usually reliable and speeds fast.

Money

Sterling, the British currency, consists of notes in denominations of £50, £20, £10 and £5, and coins worth £2, £1, 50p, 20p, 10p, 5p, 2p and 1p. A pound is 100 pence, one of which is called a penny. ATMs, known as cash machines, are plentiful in large cities, and banks will convert major currencies. Credit and debit cards are widely accepted in larger towns and cities, but small, village-based establishments are unlikely to have the facilities. If you're heading to a remote locale, take plenty of cash.

Opening hours

Shops generally operate Mon–Sat 9am–5.30pm, later in metropolitan centres. Some big supermarkets are open 24 hours. Sunday trading laws limit opening hours to six in total, usually 10am–4pm. Banks are open weekdays 9am–5.30pm, but may close earlier in small towns and on Saturday. Museums and tourist attractions usually have similar opening hours to shops, but this can vary according to season, weather, size of attraction, etc.

Passports and visas

Holidaymakers from the USA, Canada, Australia and New Zealand do not need a visa provided their stay is less than six months; South African visitors now do. Passports should have at least six months' validity. EU citizens have free movement.

Pharmacies

Pharmacies, or chemists, are well stocked and can be found in most towns. A few stay open late, until around 11pm.

Post

The rural post office is an endangered species, with many facing closure, but you will still come across them in the villages. In towns the post office is often located within the W H Smith bookshop. Look for the green-rimmed red oval (on its side) with 'Post Office' in yellow capitals. Opening hours vary widely, depending on the size and location. The service is reliable, with letters sent within the UK usually arriving the next day with a first-class stamp and within three days by second class. Airmail should arrive within three to five working days.

Public holidays

The UK's public holidays are often referred to as bank holidays. If the three fixed holidays fall on a Saturday or Sunday, the following Monday is given off in lieu.

January
1 New Year's Day
March–April
Good Friday (date varies)
Easter Monday (date varies)
May
First Monday May Day
Last Monday Spring Bank Holiday
August
Last Monday Summer Bank Holiday
December
25 Christmas Day
26 Boxing Day

Smoking

Smoking in enclosed public places is illegal under English law. This applies to restaurants, pubs, nightclubs, stations and vehicles.

Suggested reading and media

Dramatic seascapes and rugged terrain have inspired a rich seam of regional literature. The most famous local author is Daphne du Maurier (*see pp110–11*), many of whose works give a flavour of Cornwall. Winston Graham's *Poldark* series and Derek Tangye's *The Minack Chronicles* are also recommended. *Betjeman's Cornwall* is a collection of prose and poetry on the area. Devon has less of a high literary profile, but Richard Doddridge Blackmore's classic romance *Lorna Doone*, set on Exmoor, is a perennial favourite.

There is a superfluity of magazines devoted to Devon and Cornwall, and several are likely to be in your hotel room or reception. The better ones include: *Cornwall Today* (*www.cornwalltoday.co.uk*), *Inside Cornwall* (*www.insidecornwall.co.uk*), *Devon Life* (*www.devonlife.co.uk*) and the free listings guide *24-7* (*www.247magazine.co.uk*). Several local newspapers also cover the region.

Local phone codes
Exeter 01392
Falmouth 01326
Newquay 01637
Penzance 01736
Plymouth 01752
St Ives 01736
Torquay 01803
Note that 0845 and 0870 prefixes are nationwide numbers and denote a more expensive call rate. 0800 and 0808 are freephone prefixes.

Local radio, both BBC stations and commercial operators, can be handy for finding out what's on or for getting traffic updates. Useful websites include *www.visitdevon.com* *www.visitsouthdevon.co.uk* *www.visitcornwall.com*

The local village post office will take care of your post

Essentials

Telephones

Mobile phones work well in the cities and larger towns, but some remote places by the coast or on the moors have no reception whatsoever. You will still find payphones (even an iconic red one or two), where you can make calls (minimum charge 60p) and sometimes use the Internet. These often take credit and debit cards. If you're planning on making many international calls, it will be far cheaper using Skype than a payphone or – God forbid – the one in your hotel room.

Time

In summer, the UK is five to eight hours ahead of the USA, one or two hours behind South Africa, seven to nine hours behind Australia and eleven hours behind New Zealand. Daylight saving applies: clocks change on the last Sundays in March and October.

Toilets

All cafés, restaurants, hotels, petrol stations and tourist attractions have toilets, usually free of charge and in good condition. If you're caught short when you're out, café staff will often let you use their facilities.

Travellers with disabilities

Many business owners in the region have made an effort to make their premises accessible, but the situation is far from ideal. In some cases, little can be done: laws forbid most changes to listed buildings, and rugged terrain and castle nooks and crannies also present insoluble difficulties. Steep hills and narrow, pavement-less roads are another problem. With restaurants, cafés and hotels, it's worth enquiring ahead. The organisation **All Go Here** lists accessible accommodation on its website *www.everybody.co.uk*

Meanwhile, some businesses have gone the extra mile to encourage visitors with disabilities. Much of the South West Coast Path has been made accessible, and the **Dartmoor National Park Authority** publishes a booklet called *Easy Going Dartmoor* (also available online) containing information for travellers with limited mobility, and runs a dedicated tour. The **Eden Project** is another standard-bearer, with complimentary wheelchairs, plenty of seating and free admission for carers.

Emergencies

Emergency phone numbers
Fire, police and ambulance *999*
From a mobile *112*

Medical services
Casualty
There are casualty departments (also known as A&E, or Accident and Emergency) in the main towns. Emergency treatment in the UK is free to everyone, regardless of nationality.

West Cornwall Hospital
St Clare Street, Penzance.
Tel: (01736) 874000.

Derriford Hospital
Derriford Road, Crownhill, Plymouth.
Tel: 0845 155 8155.

Royal Cornwall Hospital
On the A390, next to the Treliske retail park, Truro.
Tel: (01872) 250000.

North Devon District Hospital
Raleigh Park, Barnstaple.
Tel: (01271) 322577.

Doctors
Unless it's a clear emergency, when you should dial 999, **NHS Direct** should be your first port of call, as it can advise you of the nearest medical facilities (*Tel: 0845 4647. www.nhsdirect.nhs.uk*).

You will find doctors' surgeries and dentists in most towns. Doctors and dentists operate on a register system. Patients registered with a British doctor's (GP's) surgery are treated for free. Practitioners will also treat foreigners who turn up on spec, but the consultation will be charged and you can usually claim this cost back when you return home.

Health and insurance
Travel in Devon and Cornwall is largely very safe. If you venture into the water, remember that tides can be unpredictable and the usual sea safety rules apply: stay within an appropriate distance from the shore, depending on your abilities; go with a buddy, and choose beaches with a lifeguard. The weaver fish is a nasty, sand-lurking creature with a very painful sting, which can, very occasionally, be fatal. Jelly shoes or flip-flops can help protect you. There have been serious accidents, some fatal, involving teenagers celebrating exam results and the like by 'tombstoning' – a reckless craze where people jump from great heights into water from the cliffs at Newquay. Take care near any precipices and avoid them entirely if you've been drinking.

The southwest sees the most sun in Britain, so cover up in the hottest part of the day and keep your sunscreen topped up.

The great outdoors of the national parks can also present a few hazards. They include ticks (which can be picked up in areas of dense vegetation) and the small parasite toxocara in some animal dung. The moor itself can also be hazardous for the ill-prepared, with cold temperatures presenting a real risk of hypothermia, so take advice and all the essential equipment.

Although emergency treatment is free to everyone in the UK, for anything else a foreign visitor is likely to have to pay. It is thus worth taking out adequate insurance. Remember that extreme sports, which typically include watersports, are often excluded unless you pay a premium.

Opticians
Opticians and pharmacies are run privately. Anyone can use the services and will be charged for doing so.

Safety and crime
Peaceful Cornwall and Devon have some of the lowest crime rates in the UK. Some hotels are such havens that they don't even bother to put locks on the room doors. Your main chances of an incident are in city centres at night. The British are not known for their sedateness when inebriated, and large, rowdy groups are best steered clear of. Women should try to avoid being alone in the early hours. Despite the general safety levels, the usual travelling advice – not advertising your valuables, being careful in new places and cautious of strangers – still applies.

Lost property
If you lose something at a major tourist site, or other business, enquire at the ticket desk or ask a member of staff; larger places often keep a register. To report a lost item to the Devon and Cornwall Constabulary, call 08452 777444 or go to the nearest police station.

Police
The British police are generally friendly and helpful, and can assist with day-to-day information, as well as in matters criminal. Easily recognisable, officers are dressed in dark blue or black uniforms, with white shirts and peaked cap or round bowler-style hat.

Embassies
American Embassy
24 Grosvenor Square
London W1A 2LQ
Tel: (020) 7499 9000.
http://london.usembassy.gov
Australian High Commission
Australia House, The Strand
London WC2B 4LA
Tel: (020) 7379 4334.
www.uk.embassy.gov.au
Canadian High Commission
Macdonald House
1 Grosvenor Square
London W1K 4AB
Tel: (020) 7258 6600.
www.canadainternational.gc.ca
New Zealand High Commission
New Zealand House
80 Haymarket
London SW1Y 4TQ
Tel: (020) 7930 8422.
www.nzembassy.com

Directory

Accommodation price guide

The accommodation prices are based on the cost per person for two people sharing the least expensive double room with en-suite bathroom, where appropriate. Costs vary significantly with the seasons, peaking in the summer holidays.

★ under £40
★★ £40–£80
★★★ £80–£160
★★★★ above £160

Eating out price guide

Price ranges are per person for an evening meal without drinks. Many restaurants serve set menus as well as à la carte. These are often significantly cheaper at lunchtime than in the evening.

★ under £15
★★ £15–£25
★★★ £25–£40
★★★★ above £40

NORTH DEVON

Barnstaple

ACCOMMODATION

Royal and Fortescue Hotel ★★

A former coaching inn, this hotel oozes with upmarket, genteel charm (hotel names don't come much posher), although accommodation at this central option is surprisingly affordable. The ground floor hosts a restaurant and pleasant café that's popular for Devon cream teas.
Boutport Street.
Tel: (01271) 342289.
www.royalfortescue.co.uk

EATING OUT

Old School Coffee House ★★

This traditional café serves coffee, tea and light lunches, such as toasties. The building, a former girls' school, dates from 1659.
6 Church Lane.
Tel: (01271) 372793.
Open: Mon & Wed 9.15am–3pm, Tue & Thur–Sat 9.15am–4pm.
Closed: Sun.

Clovelly

ACCOMMODATION

Red Lion ★★★

Though the bright and airy rooms are pleasant enough, it's the superlative views (of both the harbour and the sea) that get the main plaudits at the Red Lion. The restaurant is also highly regarded, and if you prefer informal dining there is pub food.
At the harbour.
Tel: (01237) 431237.
www.clovelly.co.uk

Ilfracombe

ACCOMMODATION

Ocean Backpackers ★

Popular with surfers, this independent youth hostel has a wetsuit-drying room, sea views

and free tea and coffee. As well as dormitory accommodation, you also have the choice of a family or double room.
29 St James Place.
Tel: (01271) 867835.
www.
oceanbackpackers.co.uk

EATING OUT
The Quay ★★★
Ilfracombe and Damien Hirst may appear to be strange bedfellows, but the formaldehyde shark artist has financed the restoration of a Victorian quayside building to house a modern eatery, which hosts some of his own art. The *Michelin Guide*-listed result is strong on seafood and gourmet British mains, while downstairs meals and snacks are served in the White Hart bar.
11 The Quay.
Tel: (01271) 868090.
www.11thequay.co.uk.
Open: restaurant:
Wed–Sat noon–2.30pm,
6pm–late, Sun
noon–2.30pm;

bar: Wed–Sat 10am–3pm,
6–9pm, Sun 10am–3pm.

Croyde
ACCOMMODATION
Bay View Farm ★
Family-oriented campsite (no groups allowed), with the middle field given over to couples without children. There are also caravans for hire. The site has hot showers, a washing up and laundry area, as well as a fish and chip shop.
Croyde–Barnstaple road.
Tel: (01271) 890501.
www.bayviewfarm.co.uk

SPORT AND LEISURE
Surfing Croyde Bay
As well as various courses, with group numbers kept small, this place hires and sells surfing equipment. You can replenish the energy you've expended in the water with ice cream and pastries, on sale in the shop, or at the Blue Groove, which serves sandwiches, ciabattas and baguettes, burgers, soup and drinks.

Hobbs Hill.
Tel: (01271) 891200.
www.surfingcroydebay.
co.uk

Tiverton
ACCOMMODATION
The Hartnoll Hotel ★★
With a quiet location, the hotel has 18 simple en-suite bedrooms with televisions, tea- and coffee-making facilities and Wi-Fi throughout. The cottage accommodation in the annex, which accepts pets, is suited to anyone who cannot manage the stairs in the main hotel.
Bolham.
Tel: (01884) 252777.
www.hartnollhotel.co.uk

EATING OUT
Browns ★★★
English and continental fare make up the menu at this hotel restaurant, housed in an 18th-century coaching inn. Ingredients are sourced locally, and the modern art on the wall gives the place a contemporary air.
80 West Street.
Tel: (01822) 618686.
www.brownsdevon.com.

Open: restaurant:
7.30–9.30am,
noon–2.30pm, 7–9.30pm
(Sun 8–10am); brasserie:
11am–9.30pm.

SOUTH DEVON
Exeter
ACCOMMODATION
Exeter University halls of residence ★
Available during university holidays (for a month around Easter and again from July to mid-September), the lets are on two campuses, both close to the city. Some rooms have shared bathrooms.
Tel: (01392) 215566.
www.exeter.ac.uk
Jurys Inn ★★
A quiet but central location, amiable service and pleasant, comfortable rooms make Jurys Inn a great value option.
Western Way. Tel: (01392) 312400. http://exeterhotels.jurysinns.com

EATING OUT
The Treasury ★★★
The 'no mobile phones' rule should give some clue to the classiness of this intimate hotel eatery, where the upmarket creations draw on local ingredients.
St Olaves Hotel, Mary Arches Street.
Tel: (01392) 217736.
www.olaves.co.uk.
Open: noon–2pm & 7–9pm.
Michael Caines ★★★★
Note the absence of an apostrophe – this is nothing to do with the Italian Job actor. Caines is in fact an Exeter-born top chef. Enjoying a superb location facing the cathedral, this superior restaurant serves up sophisticated modern European fare at justifiably high prices.
Abode, Cathedral Yard.
Tel: (01392) 223638.
www.michaelcaines.com.
Open: Mon–Sat noon–2.30pm & 6–10pm.

ENTERTAINMENT
Barnfield Theatre
The music ranges from jazz to a procession of tribute bands, and the theatre also stages drama, dance, comedy and other entertainment.
Barnfield Road.
Tel: (01392) 270891.
www.barnfieldtheatre.org.uk

SPORT AND LEISURE
Saddles and Paddles
As well as selling cycles (new and second-hand) and extras such as helmets, Saddles and Paddles also rents bikes and canoes, and can arrange related activities.
4 King's Wharf, The Quay.
Tel: (01392) 424241.
www.sadpad.com.
Open: summer 8.30am–6pm, winter 9am–5pm, weather dependent.

Torquay
ACCOMMODATION
Torquay Backpackers ★
With dorm-style accommodation and double rooms available, this friendly establishment is housed in a Victorian terrace.
119 Abbey Road.
Tel: (01803) 299924.
www.torquaybackpackers.co.uk

EATING OUT
Orange Tree ★★★
High-end modern European and British

fare is served in this smart eatery, with dishes such as wood pigeon, foie gras and a selection of fresh fish from nearby Brixham.
14–16 Parkhill Road. Tel: (01803) 213936. www.orangetreerestaurant. co.uk. Open: Mon–Sat 7pm–late.

ENTERTAINMENT
Little Theatre
Drama, comedy, musicals and concerts (including tribute bands galore).
St Marks Road, Meadfoot. Tel: (01803) 299330. www.toadstheatre.co.uk

South Hams
ACCOMMODATION
Park Farm ★★
Self-catering housing sleeping up to ten. The 22 hectares (55 acres) of grounds, which guests are welcome to explore, are home to cattle and sheep.
Kingsbridge. Tel: (01548) 852103. www.parkfarmbythewater. co.uk
Burgh Island Hotel ★★★★
If you're intent on pushing the boat out, this island hotel is an Art Deco gem. Individually

styled suites are named after themes and people from Mountbatten to Amy Johnson and Cunard. Facilities are what you'd expect at a venue of this calibre.
Burgh Island. Tel: (01548) 810514. www.burghisland.com

EATING OUT
TQ9 ★★★
Homely and pleasant, this hotel restaurant is heavy on local dishes, including tian of South Devon crab and rump of local lamb. The restaurant is part of a 17th-century inn. The same company runs a sister hotel in Dartmouth called the
Royal Castle (*The Quay. Tel: (01803) 833033. www.royalcastle.co.uk).
Royal Seven Stars, The Plains, Totnes. Tel: (01803) 862125. www.royalsevenstars.co.uk. Open: 6.30–9.30pm, Sun noon–2pm.*

SPORT AND LEISURE
Mountain Water Experience
Kayaking, rock climbing, abseiling, caving,

coasteering (journeying from one bay to the next along the shoreline), gorge walking and body-boarding are among the many options here for adrenalin junkies.
Courtlands, just north of Kingsbridge. Tel: (01548) 550675. www.mountain waterexperience.co.uk

Plymouth
ACCOMMODATION
Four Seasons Guest House ★★
Nothing to do with the posh international chain, the Four Seasons Guest House is a homely place marked by the hanging baskets outside. Bedrooms (five doubles and two twins, most of which are en-suite) are pleasantly done out in neutral colours. The four-course breakfast is packed with organic and local produce.
207 Citadel Road East, The Hoe. Tel: (01752) 223591. Email: fourseasonsguesthouse@ gmail.com.

www.fourseasons guesthouse.co.uk

EATING OUT

Valentis ★★

Enjoying a great spot on Plymouth Hoe, this small, friendly café serves hot and cold meals, sandwiches, ice cream as well as soft drinks and alcohol. If it's not too windy, the outside tables afford super sea views.

Hoe Lodge,
The Promenade.
Tel: (01752) 226122.
Open: 9.30am–6pm.

ENTERTAINMENT

Theatre Royal

West End musicals, opera, ballet and drama are staged in the main auditorium, while The Drum, part of the same building, hosts more experimental productions.

Royal Parade.
Tel: (01752) 668282.
www.theatreroyal.com

SPORT AND LEISURE

Discovery Surf School

Year-round surf centre offering courses with full equipment and wetsuit hire. Sister outlets can be found in Bigbury-on-Sea in Devon, and Cornwall's Whitsand Bay.

4 Belle Vue Rise, Hooe.
Tel: (07813) 639622.
www.discoverysurf.com

Sidmouth

ACCOMMODATION

Berwick House ★★

Lauded for its friendly owner, this affordable B&B comes with en-suite rooms. Housed in a 19th-century home, it's a short walk from the town centre. Rooms are small but clean. No credit cards.

Salcombe Road.
Tel: (01395) 513621.
www.berwick-house.co.uk

EATING OUT

Brophy's ★★

Cheerful café serving lunches and snack food such as sandwiches, baguettes, home-made cakes, cream teas and a range of drinks. There are newspapers to browse while you munch.

6 High Street.
Tel: (01395) 578998.
Open: Mon–Sat 9.30am–4.30pm, Sun 10am–4pm.

Beer

ACCOMMODATION

YHA Hostel ★

An atmospheric house, previously the haunt of Beer's smuggling fraternity, affords good views over the bay. This family-friendly facility also serves highly reputed food. The steep access road may prove a problem for people with limited mobility.

Bovey Combe.
Tel: 0845 371 9502.
Email: beer@yha.org.uk.
www.yha.org.uk

EATING OUT

Anchor Inn ★★–★★★

Wonderfully picturesque, whitewashed, hanging basket-bedecked hotel, whose restaurant caters for every appetite, from light snacks to full-on dinners. As you might surmise from its location (overlooking the sea), fish figures prominently, with dishes including king prawns, but there are also plenty of non-piscatorial choices such as New Zealand lamb shank and Barbary duck breast. In summer there

are barbecues in the beer garden.
Fore Street, Beer.
Tel: (01297) 20386.
www.anchorinn-beer.co.uk. Open: restaurant: Mon–Fri 7am–10pm, Sat & Sun 8am–10pm; bar: 11am–11pm.

Brixham
ACCOMMODATION
Quayside Hotel ★★★
Thirty plush en-suite rooms are decorated in warm colours and come with television and tea-making facilities. Sea views and four-poster beds incur an extra charge. Quayside has a sister hotel in Exeter (*www.queenscourt-hotel.co.uk*).
King Street.
Tel: (01803) 855751.
www.quaysidehotel.co.uk

EATING OUT
Old Market House ★★
This seafront café serves baps, baguettes, ice cream and some seafood (cockles and whelks), with indoor and outdoor seating.
4–5 Old Fish Market Buildings, The Quay.

Tel: (01803) 882484.
Open: summer 10am–about 4pm (closing time varies); winter closed.

Exmouth
ACCOMMODATION
Dolphin Hotel ★★
Centrally located and family run, Dolphin has doubles, families, twins and singles, most of which are en-suite, done out in rich reds.
2–6 Morton Road.
Tel: (01395) 263832. www.dolphinhotelexmouth.co.uk

SPORT AND LEISURE
Stuart Line Cruises
Mess about in boats of many kinds to your heart's content. While most trips depart from Exmouth, you can also sail from Topsham or Sidmouth.
5 Camperdown Terrace.
Tel: (01395) 222144 (summer); (01395) 279693 (winter). www.stuartlinecruises.co.uk

NORTH CORNWALL
Newquay
ACCOMMODATION
The Hotel ★★–★★★
Designed for the upmarket surfer, this

place draws on 'ski lodge chic' to offer trendy beachside accommodation. Families too are well provided for, with programmes and facilities for children and lower-cost, basic accommodation in a separate block, a former coach house. Four different eateries offer fresh, local produce and superb sea views; and foodies will find Jamie Oliver's Fifteen restaurant just across the car park.
On the beach, Watergate Bay.
Tel: (01637) 860543.
Email: life@watergatebay.co.uk.
www.watergatebay.co.uk
Harbour Hotel ★★★
With just five rooms, this delightful boutique hotel has impeccable personal service and luxurious touches such as Egyptian cotton bed sheets and chocolates on the pillow. Rooms are small but charming, with private balconies. The property, which is 150 years old, enjoys splendid views over the bay and there's a

mellow bar with outside terrace.
North Quay Hill.
Tel: (01637) 873040.
www.harbourhotel.co.uk

EATING OUT

Fistral Blu ★★★
A largely seafood-oriented menu, with Spanish, French and Thai-style choices among local fare, such as Cornish fish pie, with a modern twist. The venue is equally contemporary, and looks out over the beach of the same name. A new head chef is planning to add more of an Asian Fusion twist to the menu. There's a downstairs café for more relaxed bites.
Fistral Beach,
Headland Road.
Tel: (01637) 879444.
Email: info@fistral-blu.co.uk. www.fistral-blu.co.uk. Open:
noon–3pm &
6.30–9.30pm.

Fifteen ★★★–★★★★
Set up by TV chef Jamie Oliver as part of a chain of restaurants to train disadvantaged young people as chefs, Fifteen offers convivial, laid-back dining. The Cornwall outlet has a fantastic location overlooking Watergate Bay. Italian-inspired dishes are crafted from fresh, quality ingredients and served by a fun and friendly young staff. Lunchtime is busier – and cheaper. Booking is recommended in high season.
Watergate Bay.
Tel: (01637) 861000.
www.fifteencornwall.co.uk.
Open: 8.30–10.30am,
noon–4.30pm &
6.15pm–midnight. Last
orders/table bookings at
10am, 2.30pm & 9.15pm,
respectively.

SPORT AND LEISURE

Extreme Academy
The comprehensive menu of watersports on offer includes surfing, kite-surfing, paddle-surfing, wave-skiing and traction-kiting, among others. You can also hire the equipment.
Watergate Bay.
Tel: (01637) 860543.
www.watergatebay.co.uk

Fistral Beach Surf School
Flagging itself up as the only surf school on Fistral Beach, this place offers lessons for surfers of all ability levels including nil. It can also provide beach accommodation if you really want to embrace the surfer vibe.
Fistral Beach.
Tel: (01637) 850737. www.
fistralbeachsurfschool.co.uk

Padstow

ACCOMMODATION

Padstow Touring Park ★
Located about 1.5km (1 mile) from the town itself, this campsite offers electric hook-ups, private facility pitches and a sizeable children's play area. The addition of underfloor heating means the park now operates year-round. A bus route that passes the camp entrance goes to Padstow as well as the other major towns in the area.
Trerethern.
Tel: (01841) 532061.
www.padstowtouringpark.
co.uk

Treverbyn House ★★★
Two of the five colour-themed rooms at this Edwardian house, all of which are en-suite,

come with balconies.
Breakfast can be taken
in your room, in the
dining room or on the
terrace overlooking the
estuary.
*Between Treverbyn Road
& Station Road.*
Tel: (01841) 532855.
www.treverbynhouse.com

EATING OUT
Rojano's ★
If you're all fished or
Steined out, this
unpretentious and
affordable Italian trattoria
will oblige with a selection
of pizza and pasta
favourites. There's also an
outlet in Wadebridge.
9 Mill Square.
Tel: (01841) 532796.
www.rojanos.co.uk.
*Open: noon–2pm &
6pm–late.*

Stein's Fish & Chips ★★
It's not often that the
punters queue round the
block to pay the best part
of £10 for fish and chips.
But this is no ordinary
chippy. Monkfish, tiger
prawns and squid are all
on the menu, though
traditionalists will be
pleased to hear that so is
cod. Rick Stein has a
plethora of other fish

eateries and related
businesses in the town.
South Quay.
Tel: (01841) 532700.
*www.rickstein.com. Open:
noon–2.30pm & 5–9pm.*

SPORT AND LEISURE
Animal Surf Academy
Lessons for all abilities
in high season.
Polzeath.
Tel: 0870 242 2856.
www.animal.co.uk

Padstow Cycle Hire
Young, old, proficient
or beginner – this
place has a bike for
you. You can also
hire tandems, trailers
and tagalongs, and
the firm now has a
disability bike.
South Quay.
*Tel: (01841) 533533. www.
padstowcyclehire.com*

Bodmin
ACCOMMODATION
Bedknobs ★★
Three spacious and
homely rooms all come
with en-suite facilities
(including power
showers). Food is also
served.
Polgwyn, Castle Street.
Tel: (01208) 77553.
www.bedknobs.co.uk

EATING OUT
Bara Café ★
Pleasant, family-run café
serving sandwiches,
jacket potatoes, soup
and home-made cakes.
There are newspapers
to browse, a patio and
upstairs lounge. The
window seats are good
for people-watching.
14 Honey Street.
*Tel: (01208) 72206. Open:
Mon–Sat 9.30am–4.30pm
(can be later in summer).
Closed: Sun.*

Boscastle
ACCOMMODATION
Old Rectory ★★★
Outside the village
proper, this former
haunt of writer Thomas
Hardy boasts traditional
English décor, antique
furniture and roaring log
fires. If all this history is
not enough for you, the
large grounds sometimes
play host to croquet.
St Juliot.
Tel: (01840) 250225.
www.stjuliot.com

EATING OUT
Napoleon ★★
Built in 1549, Boscastle's
oldest pub ticks all the
traditional inn boxes:

barrels of beer, slate floors, log fires, oak beams, even a clome oven (a clay one with a removable clay door). There's also regular live music, bingo and a good range of locally sourced food, with a children's menu.
High Street.
Tel: (01840) 250204.
www.napoleoninn.co.uk.
Open: summer Mon–Thur 11am–2.30pm, 6pm–late, Fri–Sun 11am–late; reduced hours in winter.

Bude
ACCOMMODATION
Efford Down ⋆
Situated 1.25km (¾ mile) from the town centre, Efford Down has space for tents and a handful of camper vans. The site welcomes families and couples, but not groups. The park leads straight onto the coastal path.
On the coastal road to Widemouth Bay.
Tel: (01288) 354244.
www.efforddown.co.uk

EATING OUT
Life's a Beach ⋆⋆⋆
A superb location, international cuisine and

the most chic décor in town put this place among Bude's best. Baguettes, burgers, nachos and snacks during the day give way to posher nosh in the evening. There's disabled access as well as facilities for children.
Summerleaze Beach.
Tel: (01288) 355222.
www.lifesabeach.info.
Open: restaurant: 7pm–late; café: daily.

Port Isaac
ACCOMMODATION
Slipway ⋆⋆⋆
The simple and stylish rooms at this hotel, which dates from 1527, come with nice historical touches like exposed wooden beams. Front-facing rooms have fantastic views, some with balconies. Because it's a listed building, disabled access is limited. The same owner runs the more relaxed **Mill House Inn** (*Tel: (01840) 770200.*
www.themillhouseinn. co.uk) in the nearby village of Trebarwith.
The Harbour Front.
Tel: (01208) 880264.
www.portisaachotel.com

Tintagel
ACCOMMODATION
Pendrin House ⋆⋆
Sea views, a welcoming staff and homely rooms, some of which can host families, recommend this B&B.
Atlantic Road.
Tel: (01840) 770560.
Email:
info@pendrintintagel.co.uk.
www.pendrintingtagel. co.uk

SOUTH CORNWALL
Falmouth
ACCOMMODATION
Falmouth Lodge Backpackers ⋆
Minutes from the beach and South West Coast Path, this welcoming independent hostel has Internet access and a lounge with DVD player and games. As well as dorm accommodation in rooms sleeping up to six, you can take a double.
9 Gyllyngvase Terrace.
Tel: (01326) 319996.
www.falmouthbackpackers. co.uk
Chellowdene ⋆⋆
Open all year round, this B&B has bright and airy rooms, all of

which enjoy sea views, with two also having their own balconies. No pets, or children under ten.
Gyllyngvase Hill.
Tel: (01326) 314950.
www.chellowdene.co.uk

EATING OUT
Gurkha ★
Sticking out on the Cornish gastronomic map like a very spicy sore thumb, Gurkha offers a huge array of Nepalese and Indian dishes, including korma, tandoori and the usual complement of curries.
2A The Moor.
Tel: (01326) 311483. www. gurkhafalmouth.co.uk.
Open: noon–2.30pm & 6–10pm.

Bistro de la Mer ★★★
Popular and intimate bistro serving French favourites, from snails and mussels to an array of tempting seafood. Booking ahead is advised.
28 Arwenack Street.
Tel: (01326) 316509.
www.bistrodelamer.com.
Open: Jun–Sept Tue–Sat lunch from noon, Mon–Sun dinner from 7pm; Oct–May Tue–Sat

lunch from noon & dinner from 7pm.

ENTERTAINMENT
Princess Pavilion
Falmouth's top live events venue hosts concerts, drama, talks and exhibitions.
41 Melvill Road.
Tel: (01326) 211222.
www.carrickleisureservices. org.uk

SPORT AND LEISURE
Enterprise Boats
Cruises departing from Falmouth, Truro and St Mawes.
66 Trefusis Road, Flushing.
Tel: (01326) 374241.
www.enterprise-boats.co.uk

Land's End
ACCOMMODATION
Land's End Hotel ★★★
Large and bright individually decorated rooms, including some with four-poster beds, afford superb sea views. For location it cannot be beaten. While the ground-floor restaurant is wheelchair-accessible, the accommodation is not.

Tel: (01736) 871844.
www.landsendhotel.co.uk

Penzance
ACCOMMODATION
The Abbey ★★★
Owned and run by the family of 1960s supermodel Jean Shrimpton, the Abbey is a treasure trove of English niceties: fresh flowers, a roaring log fire and the finer points of etiquette, such as warm milk with coffee, and cold milk with tea. Parts of the property, so named because it was indeed an abbey, are around 400 years old. The restrictions on renovation (it's a listed building) result in design quirks such as a bathroom being housed in what looks like a cupboard.
Abbey Street.
Tel: (01736) 366906.
www.theabbeyonline.co.uk

EATING OUT
W C Rowe ★
This large branch of the Cornish bakery is a good place to pick up a pasty.
73 Causewayhead.
Tel: (01736) 333193.
www.wcrowe.com. Open: Mon–Sat 8am–5pm.

The Smugglers Restaurant ★★★

Quayside restaurant with views over Mount's Bay. The fish-dominated menu dresses local ingredients up with occasional international touches, in dishes from Fowey mussels with white wine to West Country sirloin steak. Though the restaurant is wheelchair-accessible, there are no disabled toilet facilities. *12–14 Fore Street, Newlyn. Tel: (01736) 331501. www.smugglersnewlyn. co.uk. Opening times vary, call to check.*

ENTERTAINMENT

Acorn Theatre

Independently run arts venue hosting a varied programme of theatre, music, dance, film, literature, poetry, talks and workshops. *Parade Street. Tel: (01736) 363545. Email: boxoffice@ acornartscentre.co.uk. www.acornartscentre. co.uk. Box office open: Tue–Sat 11am–3pm.*

Barn Club

Three-room venue that spins all sorts of tunes from mash-up and chart to dance anthems. *Eastern Green. Tel: (01736) 365754. www.barnclub.com. Open: Tue, Fri–Sun; hours vary; typically 10 or 11pm to 2 or 3am. Admission charge.*

St Ives

ACCOMMODATION

Cornerways ★–★★

Whitewashed cottage conversion, which in its former guise once hosted Daphne du Maurier (and has duly named a couple of rooms in her honour). Though close to the harbour and main museums, the location is quiet. All of the rooms have en-suite facilities. Another Cornerways can be found in Penzance (*5 Leskinnick Street. Tel: (01736) 364645. www.cornerways-penzance.co.uk*). *1 Bethesda Place. Tel: (01736) 796706. www. cornerwaysstives.com*

Garrack ★★★

This homely and comfortable family-run hotel has a gym, swimming pool, sauna and marvellous views over Porthmeor Beach. A couple of the rooms come with whirlpools and four-poster or half-tester beds. The cosy lounge has a real log fire and plenty of board games. Friendly and well appointed, the hotel restaurant (*Open: 6–9pm, Sun 12.30–1.30pm*) uses ingredients from the garden. *Burthallan Lane. Tel: (01736) 796199. www.garrack.com*

Primrose Valley Hotel ★★★

Tasteful hotel, whose individually decorated rooms boast handmade furniture and luxurious touches. Some also look out over the bay. *Porthminster Beach. Tel: (01736) 794939. www.primroseonline.co.uk*

EATING OUT

Willy Waller's Ice Cream Factory ★

Serving a quite bewildering array of flavours, Willy Waller's is to ice cream what its fictional near namesake is to chocolate.

The numerous flavours include inventive gastronomic fusions such as lavender and honey. Handmade on the premises, many of the ice creams are gluten free. There are a few tables and a bench outside.
Whitehart Buildings, 7 The Wharf.
Tel: (01736) 795761.
Open: summer 10am–10pm; winter 10am–5pm.

St Andrews Street Bistro ★★

Done out in rich colours and dotted with bohemian decorations, the contemporary British fare on the menu here jostles with North African and Middle Eastern dishes for your attention. A BYO alcohol policy adds to the value. The bistro has wheelchair access.
16 St Andrews Street.
Tel: (01736) 797074.
Open: 6–10.30pm, closed Nov & Jan.

Sport and leisure
St Ives Pleasure Boat Association
Fishing and various trips on the open wave, including Seal Island, the eponymous lighthouse of Virginia Woolf's novel *To the Lighthouse.*
Outside the lifeboat station, Wharf Road.
Tel: (07773) 008000.
www.stivesboats.co.uk

Zennor
Accommodation
Tregeraint House ★★
Warm and welcoming B&B, whose owner goes to great lengths to make guests feel at home. Just outside Zennor, Tregeraint could not be more peaceful, and its conservatory and terrace enjoy wonderful views of the surrounding countryside and sea. A log fire adds to the rustic ambience of the place.
Zennor.
Tel: (01736) 797061.
www.cornwall-online.co.uk

Eating out
The Gurnard's Head ★★
Superior pub food, where the owners' ethos is 'the simple things in life, done well'. Victuals include beer-battered hake and chips, and herb gnocchi Parisienne.
Treen, near Zennor.
Tel: (01736) 796928.
www.gurnardshead.co.uk.
Open for food: Mon–Sat 12.30–2.30pm, Sun noon–2.30pm, daily 6.30–9pm (6pm in summer).

The Lizard Peninsula
Accommodation
Blue Anchor Inn ★★
Renovated and simply furnished B&B in the centre of Helston. Large rooms, some of which are en-suite, come with television and tea- and coffee-making facilities.
50–52 Coinagehall Street, Helston.
Tel: (01326) 562821.
www.spingoales.com

Eating out
The Lizard (Ann's) Pasty Shop ★
Famous in part for the flag-burning antics of its owner (who took exception to a US food writer's vilification of the pasty), this Cornwall institution has also gained plaudits for the quality of the food. There's also a delivery service.

Sunny Corner, 3 Beacon Terrace, The Lizard, Helston.
Tel: (01326) 290889.
www.annspasties.co.uk.
Open: Easter–Oct Mon–Sat 9am–last pasty; Nov–Easter Tue–Sat 9am–last pasty. Ordering ahead advised.

Truro
ACCOMMODATION
Bay Tree Guest House ★★
Pastel colours seem to be the theme at this pretty, yellow guesthouse, a Georgian conversion with an annex. Rooms, which come with television and tea- and coffee-making facilities, sleep up to three, and bathrooms are shared.
28 Ferris Town.
Tel: (01872) 240274.
www.baytree-guesthouse.co.uk

EATING OUT
Charlotte's Tea House ★★
A celebration of Victoriana, with beamed ceilings, chandeliers and pinny-clad waitresses, Charlotte's sells a range of teas, including Earl Grey and what they bill as 'the first ever English tea grown in Cornwall', from the Tregothnan Estate. You can also get coffee, sandwiches, light meals and snacks.
Coinage Hall, 1 Boscawen Street.
Tel: (01872) 263706.
Open: Mon–Sat 10am–5pm.
Saffron ★★★
Saffron's modern British fare draws heavily on seasonal produce, its website listing the foods likely to be putting in an appearance on a monthly basis.
5 Quay Street.
Tel: (01872) 263771.
www.saffronrestaurant truro.co.uk. Open: summer Mon–Sat 10am–10pm; winter Mon 10am–3pm, Tue–Sat 10am–10pm. Closed: Sun & bank holiday Mon.

ENTERTAINMENT
Hall for Cornwall
Plays, tribute bands, musicals, the old greats and comedians all take their place on the bill here.
Back Quay.
Tel: (01872) 262465.
www.hallforcornwall.co.uk

SPORT AND LEISURE
Loe Beach Watersports Centre
Long established on the Truro scene, the centre offers tuition in sailing, windsurfing, power-boating and kayaking, plus boat and equipment hire. Activity days and a kids' club are also held.
Loe Beach, Feock.
Tel: (01872) 300800.
www.loebeach.co.uk

Polperro
ACCOMMODATION
Penryn House ★★
Simple and pleasant accommodation, all of which is en-suite and has recently been refurbished, is on offer here. Being a guest here also confers on you the rare privilege of being allowed to drive into the village.
The Coombes.
Tel: (01503) 272157.
www.penrynhouse.co.uk

EATING OUT
Couch's Great House ★★–★★★
All the sophistication and culinary verve

that you'd expect from an executive head chef who learned his craft under the tutelage of such titans of modern cuisine as Gordon Ramsay, Marco Pierre White and Raymond Blanc. Local ingredients and fish predominate. Foodies may wish to come for the gourmet tasting menu (offered Sun–Thur).
Saxon Bridge.
Tel: (01503) 272554.
www.couchspolperro.com.
Open: Mon–Sat 6.15pm–late, Sun 4.30pm–late.

Fowey
ACCOMMODATION
Old Quay House ★★★★
Ultra-stylish and elegant hotel affording fantastic estuary views. Bright and luxurious rooms come with large, comfy beds and Egyptian cotton sheets. The service is excellent, and the small touches make Old Quay House well worth the money.
28 Fore Street.
Tel: (01726) 833302.
www.
theoldquayhouse.com

EATING OUT
Q Restaurant ★★★
Award-winning eatery serving up a modern European menu, with an emphasis on seafood. Ingredients are locally sourced and the service is warm and welcoming. There are great views over the estuary.
28 Fore Street.
Tel: (01726) 833302.
www.theoldquayhouse.com.
Open: 12.30–2.30pm & 7–9pm.

St Mawes
ACCOMMODATION
Tresanton ★★★★
Demand is so high for this fabulous-looking hotel that popular rooms can book up well in advance. Some rooms have their own terraces with sea views, and there is also a public terrace.
Tel: (01326) 270055.
www.tresanton.com

EATING OUT
Tresanton ★★★–★★★★
The sophisticated menu at Tresanton's restaurant includes plenty of fish, organic veg and locally sourced meat. The floor mosaic adds to the Mediterranean feel. In warm weather, meals can be served on the terrace.
Tel: (01326) 270055.
www.tresanton.com.
Open: 12.30–2.30pm & 7–9.30pm.

GETTING AWAY FROM IT ALL
The Isles of Scilly
ACCOMMODATION
Troytown Farm ★–★★
A former flower farm, Troy Town affords splendid views and has a shop selling milk and ice cream, and seasonal meat and vegetables. Guests can camp or choose one of the self-catering options.
St Agnes.
Tel: (01720) 422360.
www.troytown.co.uk

Tresco ★★★–★★★★
A big presence on the Isles of Scilly accommodation market is Tresco, which comprises four kinds of places to bed down for the night. The plush **Island Hotel** (*Tresco. Tel: (01720) 422883*) has suites and luxury rooms with gourmet cuisine in the restaurant.

The **Flying Boat Club**
(*Tresco. Tel: (01720)
422849*) consists of
beachfront houses and
offers holidays of a more
nautical nature. The
New Inn (*Tresco.
Tel: (01720) 422844*)
is a *Michelin Guide*-listed
pub with some simple
accommodation. If
you'd rather go self-
catering, **Granite and
slate cottages**, some
by the water, some in
rural locales, sleep
between two and ten
people (*Tresco. Tel:
(01720) 422849*).
Alternatively, over
on Bryher, the large,
bright rooms of **Hell
Bay** hotel (*Bryher.
Tel: (01720) 422947*)
offer more in the way
of luxury.
www.tresco.co.uk
St Martin's Hotel ★★★★
Built to resemble granite
cottages, St Martin's
Hotel has its own quay
and leads out onto white,
sandy beaches. Rooms
are swish and the hotel
also has a restaurant as
well as bar and bistro.
*St Martin's.
Tel: (01720) 422090.
www.stmartinshotel.co.uk*

SPORT AND LEISURE
Island Sea Safaris
Diving, snorkelling (with
seals) and various boat
trips showcasing the
archipelago's wildlife
and history.
*'Nowhere', Old Town,
St Mary's.
Tel: (01720) 422732.
www.scillyonline.co.uk*

Dartmoor
ACCOMMODATION
Lydgate House ★★★
Set in 15 hectares
(36 acres) of grounds
with a river running
through, Lydgate House
enjoys a rustic location.
*Postbridge.
Tel: (01822) 880209.
www.lydgatehouse.co.uk*
Two Bridges Hotel ★★★
Over two centuries old
and sitting in 24 hectares
(60 acres) of grounds,
this impressive property
is sumptuously
furnished, with four-
poster beds, large
bathrooms replete with
statues, and chandeliers
in the dining room.
Guests include Prince
Charles and Vivien
Leigh, who met her first
husband here and has a
room named in her

honour. The Bedford
Hotel in Tavistock
(*Plymouth Road.
Tel: (01822) 613221.
www.bedford-hotel.co.uk*)
is part of the same
group, and the two host
regular murder mystery
weekends.
*Princetown.
Tel: (01822) 890581.
www.twobridges.co.uk*

EATING OUT
Gidleigh Park ★★★★
The restaurant at this
upmarket country pile
boasts two Michelin
stars. Lunch is a more
affordable option and
there is also a tasting
menu.
*Chagford.
Tel: (01647) 432367.
www.gidleigh.com. Open:
noon–2.30pm, 7–9.30pm.*

Exmoor
ACCOMMODATION
The Crown Hotel ★★★
Spacious homely and
comfortable rooms and
welcoming, obliging staff
make the countrified
Crown a peaceful base for
the exploration of
Exmoor. Food is available
in the bar (*Open: noon–
2.30pm & 7–9.30pm (Sun*

2.30pm) & 6.30–9.30pm)
and upmarket restaurant
(*Open: 7–9pm*), whose
menu is changed
seasonally. There's a
terrace and patio, with
a water garden and
pretty stream.
Exford.
Tel: (01643) 831554.
www.crownhotelexmoor.
co.uk

The Royal Oak ★★★
With its eight rooms
having been refurbished,
this 12th-century former
dairy has a cosy lounge
with a log fire, patio and
beer garden which in
summer hosts barbecues.
Thatched roofs and
touches of old-school
décor add to the bucolic
charm.
Winsford, Somerset.
Tel: (01643) 851455.
www.royaloak-
somerset.co.uk

Eating out
Andrews on the
Weir ★★★
Local seafood, Exmoor
lamb and game and
vegetarian options
are the three biggies
at this highly reputed
eatery, where locally
sourced ingredients are
fashioned into fancy fare.
Superlative coastal views
can be enjoyed while
you dine.
Porlock Weir.
Tel: (01643) 863300.
www.andrewsontheweir.
co.uk. Open: Wed–Sun
noon–2.30pm, 7–9.30pm.

Tarr Farm ★★★
Upmarket dining
geared towards the
gourmet carnivore,
with Exmoor lamb,
Devon red ruby beef,
fresh Cornish seafood,
local venison and
game plus a few veggie
options.
Tarr Steps, Dulverton.
Tel: (01643) 851507.
www.tarrfarm.co.uk.
Open: lunch noon–3pm
(Nov–Easter Mon–Fri
noon–2.30pm); coffee and
cream teas 11am–5pm,
dinner 6.30pm–late; bar
11am–late.

Bodmin Moor
Accommodation
Jamaica Inn ★★★
Daphne du Maurier
enthusiasts will be
unable to resist the
opportunity to spend a
night at the eponymous
place where she
conceived the idea for
her famous novel. The
rooms are decorated in
sympathetic style, with
four-poster beds and
other period furniture.
For a briefer visit,
there is a bar (*Open:*
summer 11am–11pm;
winter 11am–10.30pm).
Bolventor.
Tel: (01566) 86250.
www.jamaicainn.co.uk

Lavethan ★★★
If you want history,
this family-run,
grade II listed manor
house was mentioned
in the Domesday Book.
Rooms are decorated
in a traditional English
way, and you'll find
real log fires. There's
also a heated outdoor
swimming pool.
Blisland.
Tel: (01208) 850487.
www.lavethan.com

Eating out
Four Seasons ★★
This small tearoom
serves up all-day
breakfasts and other
cheap eats.
1 Market Place, Camelford.
Tel: (01840) 211779.
Open: Mon–Sat
9am–5.30 or 6.30pm,
closed Sun.

Index

Acknowledgements

Thomas Cook Publishing wishes to thank VASILE SZAKACS, to whom the copyright belongs, for the photographs in this book, except for the following images:

AA WORLD TRAVEL LIBRARY 69, 99 (K Pritchard)
KATE DENTON 123
DREAMSTIME 38 (J Kranendonk), 53 (D Hughes), 79 (C Johns), 83 (Jesse), 93 (A Hughes), 102 (R Ford), 114 (T Dobner), 117 (M Robek), 136 (R Mackenzie), 149 (E Gevaert)
EYE UBIQUITOUS/PHOTOSHOT 66, 68 (P Thomson)
GETTY IMAGES 1
MARTIN HANDFORD 151
PICTURES COLOUR LIBRARY 16, 17, 32, 44, 51, 91,
WORLD PICTURES/PHOTOSHOT 33, 34, 46, 50, 86, 92, 94

For CAMBRIDGE PUBLISHING MANAGEMENT LTD:
Project editor: Thomas Willsher
Typesetter: Donna Pedley
Copy editor: Anne McGregor
Proofreaders: Jan McCann & Jennifer Jahn
Indexer: Karolin Thomas

SEND YOUR THOUGHTS TO
BOOKS@THOMASCOOK.COM

We're committed to providing the very best up-to-date information in our travel guides and constantly strive to make them as useful as they can be. You can help us to improve future editions by letting us have your feedback. If you've made a wonderful discovery on your travels that we don't already feature, if you'd like to inform us about recent changes to anything that we do include, or if you simply want to let us know your thoughts about this guidebook and how we can make it even better – we'd love to hear from you.

Send us ideas, discoveries and recommendations today and then look out for your valuable input in the next edition of this title.

Emails to the above address, or letters to the traveller guides Series Editor, Thomas Cook Publishing, PO Box 227, Coningsby Road, Peterborough PE3 8SB, UK.

Please don't forget to let us know which title your feedback refers to!